D0982742

Human and Machine Thinking

Human and Machine Thinking

Philip N. Johnson-Laird
Princeton University

LEA LAWRENCE ERLBAUM ASSOCIATES, PUBLISHERS
1993   Hillsdale, New Jersey   Hove and London

Lawrence Erlbaum Associates, Inc., Publishers
265 Broadway
Hillsdale, New Jersey 07642

Library of Congress Cataloging in Publication Data

Johnson-Laird, P. N. (Philip Nicholas), 1936–
   Human and machine thinking / by Philip N. Johnson-Laird.
     p.   cm. — (John M. MacEachran memorial lecture series : 1990)
   Includes bibliographical references and indexes.
   ISBN 0-8058-0921-X
   1. Human information processing.   2. Thought and thinking.
   3. Artificial intelligence.   I. Title. II. Series.
   BF444.J64   1992
   153.4′3 — dc20   92-17170
                                           CIP

Printed in the United States of America
10 9 8 7 6 5 4 3 2 1

"To be a machine, to feel, to think . . ."

—La Mettrie (1748)

John M. MacEachran Memorial Lecture Series

The Department of Psychology at the University of Alberta inaugurated the MacEachran Memorial Lecture Series in 1975 in honor of the late John M. MacEachran. Professor MacEachran was born in Ontario in 1877 and received a Ph.D. in Philosophy from Queen's University in 1905. In 1906 he left for Germany to begin more formal study in psychology, first spending just less than a year in Berlin with Stumpf, and then moving to Leipzig, where he completed a second Ph.D. in 1908 with Wundt as his supervisor. During this period he also spent time in Paris studying under Durkheim and Henri Bergson. With these impressive qualifications the University of Alberta was particularly fortunate in attracting him to its faculty in 1909.

Professor MacEachran's impact has been significant at the university, provincial, and national levels. At the University of Alberta he offered the first courses in psychology and subsequently served as Head of the Department of Philosophy and Psychology and Provost of the University until his retirement in 1945. It was largely owing to his activities and example that several areas of academic study were established on a firm and enduring basis. In addition to playing a major role in establishing the Faculties of Medicine, Education and Law in the Province, Professor MacEachran was also instrumental in the formative stages of the Mental Health Movement in Alberta. At a national level, he was one of the founders of the Canadian Psychological Association and also became its first Honorary President in 1939. John M. MacEachran was indeed one of the pioneers in the development of psychology in Canada.

Perhaps the most significant aspect of the MacEachran Memorial Lecture Series has been the continuing agreement that the Department of Psychology at the University of Alberta has with Lawrence Erlbaum Associates, Publishers, Inc., for the publication of each lecture series. The following is a list of the Invited Speakers and the titles of their published lectures:

1975	Frank A. Geldard (Princeton University) "Sensory Saltation: Mestastability in the Perceptual World"
1976	Benton J. Underwood (Northwestern University) "Temporal Codes for Memories: Issues and Problems"
1977	David Elkind (Rochester University) "The Child's Reality: Three Developmental Themes"
1978	Harold Kelley (University of California at Los Angeles) "Personal Relationships: Their Structures and Processes"
1979	Robert Rescorla (Yale University) "Pavlovian Second-Order Conditioning: Studies in Associative Learning"
1980	Mortimer Mishkin (NIMH–Bethesda) "Cognitive Circuits" (*unpublished*)
1981	James Greeno (University of Pittsburgh) "Current Cognitive Theory in Problem Solving" (*unpublished*)
1982	William Uttal (University of Michigan) "Visual Form Detection in 3-Dimensional Space"
1983	Jean Mandler (University of California at San Diego) "Stories, Scripts, and Scenes: Aspects of Schema Theory"
1984	George Collier and Carolyn Rovee-Collier (Rutgers University) "Learning and Motivation: Function and Mechanism" (*unpublished*)
1985	Alice Eagly (Purdue University) "Sex Differences in Social Behavior: A Social-Role Interpretation"
1986	Karl Pribram (Stanford University) "Brain and Perception: Holonomy and Structure in Figural Processing"
1987	Abram Amsel (University of Texas at Austin) "Behaviorism, Neobehaviorism, and Cognitivism in Learning Theory: Historical and Contemporary Perspectives"
1989	Robert S. Siegler and Eric Jenkins (Carnegie Mellon University) "How Children Discover New Strategies"
1991	Timothy A. Salthouse (Georgia Institute of Technology) "Mechanisms of Age–Cognition Relations in Adulthood"
1992	Philip N. Johnson-Laird (University of Alberta) "Human and Machine Thinking"

Eugene C. Lechelt, Coordinator
MacEachran Memorial Lecture Series

Sponsored by The Department of Psychology, The University of Alberta with the support of The Alberta Heritage Foundation for Medical Research in memory of John M. MacEachran, pioneer in Canadian psychology.

Contents

Prologue

What is thinking? One answer is that it is what intervenes between perception and action. If it intervenes too much, then action may be postponed indefinitely: prudence in excess is paralysis, but thinking normally leads from one mental representation of the world to another in order to prepare the individual for the demands of life. This answer, from Kenneth Craik (1943), lies at the heart of *Functionalism,* the doctrine that what is crucial to thinking is not the physical make-up of the brain, not nerve, synapse, and neurotransmitter, but the organization and functioning of mental processes and representations. Of course, a knowledge of the neural processes of the brain may help us to understand the functional organization of thinking.

The simplest organisms, such as bacteria and protozoa, react physically to their immediate environment. A paramecium, for example, is a single-celled organism that swims through the water by the coordinated beating of its hairlike cilia. If it bumps into an obstacle, it backs off, and then swims away in a different direction. It is tempting to suppose that it has determined that its way is blocked and decided to set a different course. In fact, it forms no representation of the external world, and thinks not at all. The bump depolarizes its cell membrane, the ensuing chemical changes cause its cilia to reverse the direction of their power strokes, and so it swims in a reverse direction. As the membrane recovers, normal swimming resumes, with a probable change in course. The organism appears to move in a thoughtful way, but in reality it neither represents the world nor has any mental life.

Evolution has produced creatures with nervous systems that detect patterns of energy from distant objects and that can use such patterns to construct an internal representation of the external world. These representations, as Craik pointed out, are the basis for inferences about future states of the world and decisions about appropriate actions. But what are mental representations? They cannot be distinguished by their ultimate medium, because all biological processes—both those that form representations and those that do not—depend on protein molecules. Their essential characteristic is accordingly their functional role: a causal chain leads from an object, A, to a pattern of energy impinging on an organism's sensory organs; these devices convert the energy into nerve impulses, and from them the brain constructs a further pattern, A', in an internal symbolic notation that can be used to control action. The representation will be useful to the extent that it covaries with the state of the world and makes explicit those aspects of it that are relevant to action. The organism can avoid an obstruction, A, by virtue of the representation, A'.

Christopher Longuet-Higgins has devised a beautiful demonstration of the functional essence of representations. A simple robot moves around on top of a table. Whenever it is about to fall off, it rings an alarm bell to summon its human keeper. The robot has neither an electronic camera nor any sort of pressure sensors, so how can it possibly perceive the edge of the table? The answer turns—literally—on a representation. The robot has two main wheels, one on the middle of each side, which drive two smaller wheels that hold a piece of sandpaper up beneath its baseplate. The paper is the same shape as the table. As the small wheels turn, they move the paper around beneath the baseplate so that at any moment their position on the paper corresponds to the position of the robot on the table. When the small wheels reach the edge of the paper, a circuit is closed to ring the alarm bell. The main wheels are, thus, both a means of transport and perceptual organs registering the robot's movement around the table. The position, A, of the robot corresponds to the position, A', of the smaller wheels on the paper, and this position governs the robot's action of sounding the alarm. In short, the robot has a rudimentary representation of its position on the table-top.

Unlike the robot, a human being is equipped with sensory organs that convert energy into nerve impulses and a brain that processes this information. The transformation of energy into nerve impulses depends on physical processes; so, too, does the subsequent processing that constructs a representation. Yet, there is a crucial difference. The interaction between light and the visual pigment in the cells of the retina is only a physical process. The construction of a representation depends on a symbolic notation. Many such notations are possible, but evolution has fixed on a particular one. From a functional standpoint, the choice was arbitrary, that is, a different notation would have worked as well, just as a different size of wheels and sandpaper in the right proportions would have allowed the robot to work as well. The use of an arbitrary notation in this sense is an essential characteristic of a special class of devices, a class that can be described as *computational, information-processing,* or *symbol-manipulating*—the terms are interchangeable. Sensing energy and using nerve impulses to release the energy for muscle contractions are both physical processes. Between these two processes, however, is the mind, and the mind is an information-processing device that makes and manipulates symbolic representations of the world (see, e.g., Craik, 1943; Miller, Galanter, & Pribram, 1960; Newell & Simon, 1972). The meeting of minds through overt symbolic communication among individuals is, of course, the supreme agent of human culture and social convention.

Some theorists reject the view that thinking is the manipulation of internal representations. Thus, Husserl, the founder of a philosophical movement known as phenomenology, rejected the very idea of mental representations of the world. The relation of thinking to its object is immediate, he held, and does not occur by way of some mental symbol (see Husserl, 1929). Other more recent thinkers also reject the information-processing analysis of mental phenomena (e.g., Edelman, 1987; Gibson, 1966). One way to try to rebut these theorists is to construct an a priori case for mental representations, perhaps along the lines just sketched. Such arguments are never decisive, however, and sooner or later a functionalist must abandon the endless rearrangement of leaves in the philosophical album and enter the psychological laboratory to test a theory of thinking based on mental representations.

Where should one begin to search for a theory? One answer is in the study of the brain. Unfortunately, however, neuroscientists have so far discovered hardly anything about the neural mechanisms of thinking. Similarly, cognitive neuropsychologists have barely begun to investigate the effects of brain damage on thinking. Hence, at present, a theory of thinking must be based on psychological studies. Figure 1, which I have borrowed from an earlier work, lays out a taxonomy of thinking in terms of some major distinctions: Is the thought process governed by a goal, as in solving a problem? Is it deterministic, in that what happens next depends only on the current state of the system and its input? Does it have a precise goal—as in testing the validity of an inference—or is it merely constrained by general factors, as in creating a work of art? Does it increase semantic information or not?

As the figure shows, the gamut of human thinking runs all the way from the calculations of mental arithmetic to the association of ideas. Mental arithmetic is not an ideal arena to search for a general theory of thinking. It is highly specialized, and based on deterministic procedures that are taught in the classroom, although explanations of the ability are surprisingly diverse. Association is more representative, but ironically, it is too

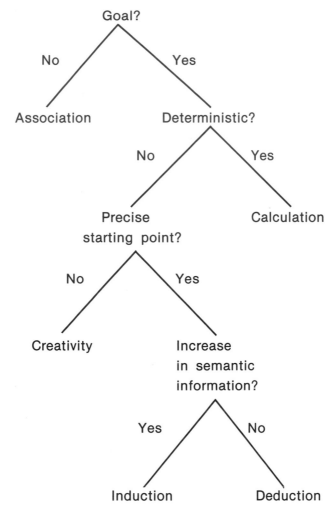

FIG. 1. A taxonomy of thinking (from Johnson-Laird, 1988a).

hard to understand. One thought can lead associatively to another in dreams and daydreams (Mueller, 1990; Singer, 1978). Despite its long-standing study, however, there is no adequate theory of this process of how one idea can lead to another in a way that seems "unguided, and without design" (Hobbes, 1651/1968). There may be stored associative links between words, but the dreamwork cannot consist in the unfolding of existing associations between ideas. If that were so, it would never lead to a *novel* idea.

Neither calculation nor association is most typical of human thinking. They are extremes—the clocks and clouds of the mind—and so the search for a theory should begin with what lies between them, with those modes of thinking (deduction, induction, and creation) that are carried out by both humans and machines.

Why machines in this context? There are two reasons. The first is that we have never fully understood a process until we can build a machine to carry it out. The second is that machines think—they think the way in which we think that we think. In fact, machines are so stupid that the way we think that we think cannot possibly be correct. The reason that we are so wrong, I suspect, is because our theories of thinking reflect our consciousness, not the underlying machinery on which it depends. There is a difference between conscious, cold-blooded and logical theories of thinking and tacit mental processes. One of my aims is to bring out this difference.

You may wonder why I am so certain about the stupidity of our machines. The answer is that they have not yet devised theories of how they think that they think, yet we understand them well. This point brings out the fundamentally recursive nature of psychology: the more clever a theory of thinking, the still cleverer it needs to be in order to explain its own origins. Psychology is the only discipline that puts forward theories that need to explain how they themselves came into being. Bertrand Russell once remarked that in a democracy the people are always more stupid than their leaders: the more stupid the leaders, the still more stupid the people for having elected them. In psychology, alas, our theories tend to be more stupid than we are.

Do machines really think? Surely not, skeptics say: the notion is an absurdity. Just as surely, functionalists retort, machines can think if they have the right representations and processes. Machines *do* think, materialists such as La Mettrie (1748/1912) confirm, because human beings think, and human beings are machines. Alan Turing, redoubtable functionalist and founder of the theory of computability, framed his famous "imitation game" as a way out of this controversy. The question "Can machines think?," he wrote (Turing, 1950), requires one to define the meaning of the terms *machine* and *think*. Instead of attempting such definitions, he chose to replace the question by a problem related to it but less ambiguous:

The problem arises from a game that is played by three people: a man, a woman, and an interrogator, who are in separate rooms. The object of the game is for the interrogator to determine which of the other two is the man and which is the woman. The interrogator puts questions to them and they reply by teleprinter. The man's task is to try to deceive the interrogator; the woman's task is to try to help the interrogator. As Turing wrote: "We now ask the question, 'What will happen when a machine takes the part of [the man] in this game?' Will the interrogator decide wrongly as often when the game is played like this as he does when the game is played between a man and a woman? These questions replace our original, 'Can a machine think?' "

Alas, the imitation game will not do: it is time to retire Turing's test. One of its shortcomings can be illustrated by the dilemma of a chess-playing friend of mine. The oddity of his opponent's moves in a game played by mail convinced him that he was playing a computer program, not a human being. I checked whether the moves matched those of a chess-playing program that runs on principles remote from human psychology. In fact, the program predicted my friend's moves better than it predicted his opponent's moves. Thus, here is a case in which a person fails Turing's test and is falsely taken for a computer, and a program passes the test and is falsely taken for a person.

Any scientific theory, as far as we know, can be modeled in a computer program. Whether that program *embodies* the phenomenon is a very different matter. A computer model of the country's economy is certainly not to be confused with the economy itself. Imagine, however, a more advanced robot than Longuet-Higgins's table-top device, one that is equipped with an electronic camera and software that constructs a representation of the external world. Imagine, further, that to fulfill its goals, the robot has a program that enables it to construct representations of likely future states of the world, and to use them to determine its course of action. Such a robot, I say, perceives, thinks, and acts. Of course, it may not do any of these tasks very well: its methods may be crude, stupid, and remote from their human counterparts. So, too, are the methods of other species, such as rats and pigeons. Hence, the critical question is: "Can a machine think in the same ways that a human being does?" The answer will be found, not by some form of imitation game, but by developing a robust *theory* of human thinking, and showing that it can, or cannot, be implemented in a machine. One day, programs that think in a human way may be devised, but existing programs fall short of human thought. Some of these programs are works of artificial intelligence; others are designed to model theories of human thinking. They simulate processes of deduction, induction, and creation, but they do not yet embody them.

Computer models of thinking exorcise problems that have haunted psychological theorizing. One such problem is too exclusive a focus on error. Many theories describe what creates difficulties in thinking, but fail to explain normal competence. A classic example is the so-called "atmosphere" hypothesis in deductive reasoning, according to which the premises of a deduction can create a purely superficial atmosphere that favors a certain form of conclusion. For instance, both of the following premises contain the quantifier *all*:

All the athletes are bodybuilders.
All the canoeists are bodybuilders.

Therefore, they are supposed to create an atmosphere favorable to a conclusion containing *all*:

All the athletes are canoeists.

Woodworth and Sells (1935), and other more recent theorists, argued that people sometimes reason correctly and sometimes succumb to this atmosphere effect. The claim may be true, but it tells us nothing about the process of correct reasoning. A proper theory should explain both basic competence and the causes of error. Computer modeling makes it harder for theorists to neglect such an integrative framework.

A second problem is vagueness. By this, I mean theorizing that uses concepts so vague or mystifying that one cannot be certain of grasping their content unless one has the opportunity to interrogate the theorizer personally. Even then, the answer may not be clear. A sure sign of vague psychological theorizing is the existence of pedagogical works that purport to explain what X's theory really means. Any theory must take some concepts for granted, but it should not take too much for granted. The need can be met by ensuring that the resulting theory is computable. Computability is well understood, and its explicit mathematical foundation takes for granted only a handful of simple concepts (which I explain further on). Moreover, the construction of a computer model almost always leads to significant improvements in the theory itself.

Of course, computer modeling is not without dangers of its own. Programs are complex, and their descriptions are often beyond comprehension. They may embody a vast set of ad hoc procedures patched together to yield a seemingly impressive performance. The antidote to mystification by computer modeling is to insist on three principles.

1. Psychological theories and the computer programs that model them must be kept distinct: the program is *not* the theory, because its implementation will inevitably depend on many arbitrary decisions. These are needed to make the program work, but are not motivated by the theory.

2. There must be separate descriptions of *what* the program computes and of *how* it works. Too many programs are described without any separate account of what they are supposed to compute.

3. Computer models of cognitive processes invariably finesse many problems, and operate for only limited domains. Both of these restrictions are entirely proper for a model, but they should be clear to readers.

The goals of this book are to reach an understanding of how the mind carries out three sorts of thinking—deduction, induction, and creation—to consider what goes right and what goes wrong, and to explore computational models of these sorts of thinking. The book is aimed at students of the mind—psychologists, computer scientists, philosophers, linguists, and other cognitive scientists—but it is intended to provide general readers with a self-contained account of human and machine thinking. My aim has been to present not a review, but a point of view. I have tried to keep things as simple as possible, and to provide a self-contained book that does not require any technical background. I hope that it is as much fun, and as intellectually challenging, as the field of research itself. What both call for is hard thinking (about thinking).

* * *

This book was inspired by an invitation from Professor Eugene Lechelt to deliver the MacEachran Memorial Lectures in the Department of Psychology at the University of Alberta, Edmonton. To try to meet the separate demands of text and lecture, I wrote a draft of the book, derived the gist of the lectures from it, and finally rewrote it after the lectures had been delivered in October, 1990. Much of the work that I report was collaborative. Chapter 1 is based almost entirely on research carried out jointly with Ruth M.J. Byrne, now of the Department of Psychology, Trinity College, Dublin. I am grateful to her for allowing me to make use of this research. My thanks, also, to some long-standing groups of friends and collaborators: Bruno Bara of the University of Florence, Alan Garnham and Jane Oakhill of the University of Sussex, Paolo Legrenzi of the University of Trieste, Keith Oatley of the Ontario Institute of Science and Education in Toronto, Patrizia Tabossi of the University of Bologna, and the founder of the modern study of deductive reasoning, Peter Wason of University College London.

Professor Lechelt and his colleagues were wonderful hosts at Edmonton. Peter Dixon and Fernanda Ferreira gave up precious time to look after my wife and me. They, together with Mike Dawson, Alinda Friedman, John Henderson, and other members of the department ensured that we enjoyed a memorable stay. My thanks, also, to the audience at the lectures who asked thought-provoking questions and to the informal group who adjourned to the bar after each lecture to pursue the answers as far as we could go.

I must also thank those who helped me to write this book. Over the years, Sam Glucksberg, John Darley, and Joel Cooper cumulatively persuaded me to move to the Department of Psychology at Princeton University. They were more than abetted by George Miller, who in a long collaboration, has taught me more cognitive science than I can remember. They and their colleagues generate a highly stimulating and congenial atmosphere for research. A number of friendly critics have read the book in draft form: I thank Earl (Buz) Hunt, my colleague Eldar Shafir, and an anonymous reader for their helpful admonitions and corrections. Nancy Nersessian and Paul Thagard similarly gave me the benefit of their advice on the problem of the incommensurability of scientific theories. As ever, Larry Erlbaum and Judi Amsel remain all that publishers should be: generous, supportive, and good company. (They are also an enthusiastic audience for my efforts to play modern jazz piano.) Finally, Mo, Ben, and Dorothy have helped, cajoled, and administered psychotherapy whenever called for. My whole-hearted thanks to every one of these individuals. The book may not receive their imprimatur, but it is the better for their interest and encouragement.

— Philip N. Johnson-Laird

1 Deduction

There is a story, perhaps apocryphal, that the famous philosopher, Ludwig Wittgenstein, once became embroiled in a profound discussion with a colleague on the platform at the Cambridge railway station. The guard blew his whistle, but they were oblivious until the train began to trundle away, whereupon Wittgenstein raced after it with the colleague in his wake. He leapt aboard perilously, but she was left behind disconsolate on the platform. "Never mind, love," said a sympathetic porter, "There'll be another train along in 10 minutes".

"But you don't understand," she replied, "He was seeing *me* off."

The porter's inference is a typical everyday deduction. It depends on perception and general knowledge. He made the following observation:

She's running after the train.

and he assumed:

If she's running after the train, then she's trying to catch it.

And so he concluded:

She's trying to catch the train.

The deduction is *valid;* that is, the conclusion must be true if the premises are true. If the premises are not true, however, then there is no guarantee that the conclusion is true. In fact, the premises in this case are true, and

Wittgenstein's colleague was indeed trying to catch the train (and to prevent him from doing so).

The ability to think rationally is central to human life. You have certain beliefs and certain desires and needs: to attain these goals, you must infer from your beliefs what you have to do in order to attain them and then carry out those actions. Your beliefs need to be true more often than not, and so do the conclusions that you infer. If any skeptic denies this story and extols irrationality, then, in the words of Jerry Fodor: "Don't listen to what they say; watch what they do." When they want to catch trains, they run after them; when they want to make inferences about such events, they are able to do so.

At the heart of rationality is the capacity to make valid deductions; the goal of this chapter is to discuss how human beings exercise this capacity, and how they have designed machines to do so. People have assumed almost without reflection that deduction depends on formal logic. The advantage of this assumption is that it obviates the tricky problems of meaning. Nothing is more natural for a machine than the mechanical manipulation of uninterpreted symbols, and, as the great 17th-century German mathematician and logician, Gottfried Leibniz, recognized, nothing is more helpful in the dispassionate analysis of arguments than calculations that concern form, not content. Yet, I shall argue that everyday human reasoning is not a formal syntactic process. It is, instead, a matter of understanding meanings and manipulating their mental representations.

The chapter begins with logic because that is where one finds a clear distinction between syntax and semantics, that is, between form and meaning. It then turns to psychology and considers theories of reasoning: first, those based on formal rules of inference, and next, those based on the semantic process of constructing models. I contrast these two approaches in the light of experimental evidence about human reasoning, and finally draw a lesson for those who design deductive machines.

Logic, Form, and Validity

Logic is the intellectual discipline concerned with the validity of deductions. Many people suppose that the only way to demonstrate that an argument is valid is to derive a formal proof of it in a logical calculus. They are mistaken. Logicians distinguish between such *proof-theoretic* methods, which depend on formal rules of inference, and *model-theoretic* methods, which depend on a semantic way to demonstrate validity.

To construct a formal proof of an argument, such as:

> If she was running after the train, then she was trying to catch it.
> She was running after the train.
> ∴ She was trying to catch it.

the first stage is to establish the *logical form* of the argument, namely:

If p then q
p
∴ q

where p and q, which correspond to elementary propositions, are hence-forth treated as uninterpreted symbols and ∴ means therefore. The next stage is to find an appropriate sequence of formal rules that lead, step by step, from premises to conclusion. In so-called "natural deduction" systems of logic, each connective has its own rules of inference. Hence, the following formal rule of *modus ponens* can be used with a conditional premise:

If A then B
A
∴ B

where A and B are any propositions whatsoever. Because this rule matches the logical form of the argument in the example, it suffices to prove the conclusion. In more complicated cases, a derivation calls for a series of steps, each sanctioned by a formal rule, and one searches for the right steps in the "space" of all possible derivations from the premises (as we shall see in the example presented further on of a proof by *reductio ad absurdum*).

Validity depends on truth and, in particular, on the set of possible situations in which the premises would be true. To establish the validity of an argument by semantic means, one needs to show that the conclusion holds true for any possible situation in which the premises are true. It does not matter if the premises are false in the actual world: validity means that *if* they were true, then the conclusion would be true, too. Likewise, it is not enough to establish merely that the premises and conclusion are true in the actual world. That relation could be a coincidence, and in other circumstances the premises might have been true and the conclusion false. A semantic test of validity therefore calls for an exhaustive analysis of all possibilities. It depends on the meanings of the premises and accordingly on the meanings of the connectives they contain. In everyday language, such connectives as *if, and,* and *or,* can go beyond strictly logical meanings to express, say, temporal relations. Conjunction, for example, often implies a temporal order, as shown by the contrast between: "They got married and had a baby" and "They had a baby and got married." We will ignore such usages here, although they can be accommodated by semantic methods, and analyze the purely logical meanings of connectives.

The process of testing validity by a semantic method can be illustrated using the railway porter's deduction. Its premises contain two elementary (or *atomic*) propositions: She was running after the train; she was trying to catch the train. Given that any proposition is either true or false, then there are just four possible combinations of truth values for these two propositions, which are shown in the following truth table:

She was running after the train.	She was trying to catch the train.
True	True
True	False
False	True
False	False

Each row in the table corresponds to a separate possibility, e.g., the first row corresponds to the situation in which both propositions are true. The first premise of the deduction is the conditional:

If she was running after the train, then she was trying to catch it.

It rules out as impossible the situation corresponding to the second row in the table: if the conditional is true, then it is impossible for both its antecedent, "She was running after the train", to be true and its consequent, "She was trying to catch the train", to be false. The second premise:

She was running after the train.

similarly eliminates the situations corresponding to the third and fourth rows. Hence, all that remains is the first row:

She was running after the train.	She was trying to catch the train.
True	True

When you have eliminated the impossible, as Sherlock Holmes remarked, then whatever remains, however improbable, must be the case. What must be true in this case is that the woman was trying to catch the train. There is no situation in which the premises are true and this conclusion is false. The semantic method shows that deduction is valid.

The semantic method depends on principles for constructing truth tables and for eliminating rows from them according to the meanings of the premises, and particularly the meanings of the propositional connectives, *not, if, and,* and *or.* It makes no use of formal rules of inference such as *modus ponens.* For propositional connectives, however, logicians have shown that if a deduction is valid according to the semantic method then it can be proved in a calculus based on formal rules, and vice versa.

Some deductions depend not merely on propositional connectives but also on quantifiers, such as *none, any,* and *some.* The following valid deduction is an example:

> If any person is running after any other person then the former is trying to catch the latter.
> Someone is running after Ludwig.
> ∴ Someone is trying to catch Ludwig.

Such a deduction can be proved in the predicate calculus, which supplements the formal rules for connectives with formal rules for quantifiers. These rules are described later in the chapter (in the section on reasoning with multiply quantified relations). Once again, a deduction is valid if its conclusion is true in any possible situation in which its premises are true. Logicians generally work with models, which are abstract mathematical objects, rather than with real situations. Because an assertion such as, "Someone is running after Ludwig," can be true in a potentially infinite number of different situations, no method could work by directly inspecting all possible models. One system of formal rules of inference, however, emulates the elimination of models: the *semantic tree* method for the predicate calculus (Beth, 1971). In the propositional calculus, all and only the semantically valid inferences are derivable in formal proofs. The same holds for the predicate calculus, but it is only "semi-decidable": that is, if a deduction is valid, then in principle a formal derivation for it can be found, but if it is invalid, then the search may go into an endless loop, so its invalidity may never be proved.

Logicians developed formal calculi on the basis of their semantic intuitions, but a long time elapsed until they were able to make these intuitions precise in a semantic theory. Frege published an account of the predicate calculus in 1879; Tarski did not publish a systematic theory of its semantics until 1936. This hiatus may explain the overwhelming bias of theorists toward accounts of human and machine reasoning based on formal rules of inference. Formal proof and semantic validity differ in principle, however. The wedge between them was driven into place by the greatest logician of the 20th century, Kurt Gödel (1931/1967), who showed that there are true assertions in arithmetic that cannot be proved in a consistent formal calculus. Within a formalization of arithmetic, he was able to provide a general recipe for constructing arithmetical assertions that have a very peculiar property: they assert of themselves that they are not provable within the formalization. Such an assertion is either true or false. If it is true, then indeed there is a true arithmetical assertion that cannot be formally proved. If it is false — that is, the assertion can be proved — then the formalization is inconsistent because it allows the proof of an assertion that asserts its own unprovability. In short, there are arithmetical truths that cannot be proved in a consistent formalization of arithmetic. Gödel's so-called "incompleteness" theorem brought to an end the formalist program in logic. Semantic validity cannot be reduced to syntactic proof.

FORMAL RULES OF INFERENCE

Formal Rules in the Mind

The task of making a deduction can be divided into three main stages:

1. Understanding: reasoners must grasp the starting point of the deduction, which may be a set of verbal premises, a situation that they can perceive, imagine, or remember, or some mixture of these sources of information.
2. Generating a conclusion: they must generate a putative conclusion unless someone—a helpful psychologist perhaps—provides them with one.
3. Evaluating the conclusion: if reasoners are prudent, they should submit the putative conclusion to critical evaluation to determine whether or not it follows validly from the premises.

According to formal theories of human reasoning, the first stage consists in extracting the logical form of the premises, and representing it in a way that dovetails with the mental representation of the formal rules of inference. Despite the efforts of many logicians and linguists, no complete account exists of either the logical form of sentences or of how that form is extracted from them. Inferences based on perception need the content of the perception translated into a logical form. Again, however, there is no account of how reasoners extract such representations from their perceptual observations. Formal theories of reasoning, therefore, have had little to say about the first stage of the process. They have also, until recently, had little to say about the second stage: the generation of conclusions. An important problem, often overlooked by psychologists (e.g., Inhelder & Piaget, 1958), is that logic supports an infinite number of valid conclusions from any set of premises, and does not stipulate which particular conclusion should be drawn. These valid conclusions include, for example, a conjunction of all the premises, a conjunction of a premise with itself some arbitrary number of times, and other equally trivial cases. People who are sane (other than logicians) do not draw such conclusions, but formal theories do not account for the conclusions that they do draw.

The main emphasis in formal theories is on the third stage, and many theorists, beginning with the Swiss student of children's intellectual development, Jean Piaget, have argued that it depends on a tacit formal calculus. It might seem surprising that mere human beings are supposed to develop a formal calculus that logicians construct with great effort. Nevertheless, the idea of formal rules in the mind has attracted many adherents (e.g., Braine, 1978; Osherson, 1974–1976; Pollock, 1989; Sperber & Wilson, 1986). The following characteristic formulation of deduction from Rips (1983), captures the central assumption of the formalist approach and its emphasis on the evaluation of given conclusions: "Deductive reasoning consists in the application of mental inference rules to the premises and conclusion of an argument. The sequence of applied rules forms a mental derivation or proof of the conclusion from the premises where these implicit proofs are analogous to the explicit proofs of elementary logic."

In general, formalists predict the difficulty of a deduction in terms of two principles: First, the longer the derivation, the harder the inference, and, second, certain rules are harder to use, or less accessible, than others. In some cases, the postulated rules allow a conclusion to be derived in a single step. Thus, most theories postulate that the rule of *modus ponens,* already described, is part of mental logic. In other cases, a chain of deductions has to be constructed and may depend on reasoning by supposition. Consider the following example:

> If she was running after the train, then she was trying to catch it.
> She was not trying to catch the train.
> ∴ She was not running after it.

It has the following form:

> if p then q
> not q
> ∴ not p

According to most formal theories (e.g., Braine, 1978; Osherson, 1974–1976; Rips, 1983), mental logic contains no rule for this deduction, which is of a form known as *modus tollens.* Hence, it must proceed from a supposition:

> p   (by hypothesis)

The rule of *modus ponens* applied to this hypothesis and the first premise yields:

> q

This conclusion can be conjoined with the second premise to yield:

q & not q

but this conjunction is a self-contradiction, and so the hypothesis from which it is derived must be rejected according to the rule of *reductio ad absurdum:*

∴ not p

The theory predicts, of course, that this deduction should be harder than *modus ponens* because it depends on a longer derivation.

Some typical formal rules postulated in various theories (e.g., Braine, Reiser, & Rumain, 1984; Rips, 1983) include the following:

A	
B	A and B
∴ A and B	∴ A
	A or B
A	not-B
∴ A or B	∴ A
	If A then B
A ⊢ B (i.e., B can be derived from A)	A
∴ If A then B	∴ B

The rules on the left are used to introduce connectives into arguments, and the rules on the right are used to eliminate them from arguments.

Formal theories have been investigated experimentally by asking subjects to evaluate given conclusions, or to rate the difficulty of large batteries of deductions (see Rules Versus Models, further on). The data are then fitted by estimating post hoc the accessibility of each of the postulated formal rules of inference. The results have been quite successful, but limited to propositional inferences and simple relational inferences. No comprehensive formal rules for reasoning with quantifiers have been proposed by psychologists.

Formal Rules in Machines

Most programs for machine reasoning represent the logical form of an argument (together with axioms for any relevant general knowledge) and then search for a derivation of the conclusion based on the formal rules of a logical calculus. Some of these programs are frank attempts to model human performance (e.g., Newell, Shaw, & Simon, 1963). Some are exercises in artificial intelligence (e.g., Robinson, 1979). Some are intended as automated reasoning systems that will help human users to find proofs (e.g., Wos, 1988). Which of the infinitely many valid conclusions should a program draw? Like psychologists, programmers finesse this problem. Almost all the programs require conclusions to be provided by the human user: they search for derivations of given conclusions rather than generate conclusions of their own. The main issues have been which system of rules of inference to use and how to control the search for derivations. One option is to adopt a *natural deduction* system, similar to those advocated by psychologists, in which each connective has its own rules of inference (e.g., Bledsoe, 1977; Reiter, 1973). An alternative is to use only a single rule of inference, the "resolution" rule, or one of its many variants. The simplest form of the rule is:

    A or B
    not-A or C
∴ B or C

The rule exploits the fact that all propositional connectives can be re-expressed in terms of inclusive disjunction and negation: for example, if p then q is treated as equivalent to the inclusive disjunction, not-p or q, because both are false only if p is true and q is false. Other special procedures are used to eliminate quantifiers. In particular, the quantifier *any* can simply be dropped from an expression. Hence, a premise such as:

For any x, if x is a psychologist then x is an experimenter.

is transformed into a logically equivalent disjunction from which the quantifier has been dropped:

x is a not a psychologist or x is an experimenter.

The process of *unification* allows the value of a variable to be set to a value that occurs in another expression that has the same predicate. Thus, for example, the following two expressions can be unified:

x is an experimenter.
Mary is not an experimenter.

by setting the value of x equal to Mary. The resolution rule applies to the following premises because the two italicized clauses can be unified:

x is a not psychologist or *x is an experimenter.*
Mary is not an experimenter or Mary is a statistician.

and it cancels out the two italicized clauses to leave behind:

Mary is a not psychologist or Mary is a statistician.

or, in other words:

If Mary is a psychologist then she is a statistician.

The formal derivation of a deductive conclusion resembles the execution of a computer program, and the analogy is exploited in *logic programming.* Languages, such as PROLOG, have been developed in which computation is analogous to a proof that a statement follows from others in a fragment of the predicate calculus (see Clocksin & Mellish, 1981). The programmer formulates a set of declarative statements that characterizes both a problem and the constraints on its solution; computation consists of a search for a solution based on a form of resolution theorem proving.

Even with a single formal rule, such as resolution, there is a choice of assertions to which the rule should be applied, and the number of potential candidates increases as more and more interim conclusions are derived. In practice, even the search for a relatively simple derivation of half a dozen lines may require thousands of lines of derivation to be explored (see Wos, 1988). Machines programmed using natural deduction systems run into the same problem of intractability, and, as Pelletier (1986) pointed out, they may even be unable to make certain deductions, including proofs of simple tautologies. Here are some examples, which are presented with a summary of Pelletier's comments:

1. $((p \rightarrow q) \rightarrow p) \rightarrow p$ — Unprovable by Newell and Simon's (1972) program.

2. $((p \lor q) \rightarrow (p \lor r)) \rightarrow (p \lor (q \rightarrow r))$ — Judged by Siklossky, Rich, & Marimov (1973) to be the hardest of the first 67 theorems of Whitehead and Russell (1910).

3. $((p \& (q \rightarrow r)) \rightarrow s) \leftrightarrow ((\neg p \lor q \lor s) \& (\neg p \lor \neg r \lor s))$ — A problem that appears not to be provable by Bledsoe, Boyer, & Heaneman's (1972) program.

The symbols denote the standard propositional connectives:

"¬" for *not*
"&" for *and*
"v" for inclusive *or*
"→" for *if*
"↔" for *if and only if*

Formal Rules and Non-Monotonic Reasoning

There is a further difficulty for formal rules. The following trivial deduction is valid:

>   Arthur is a person.
>   Persons have two legs.
> ∴ Arthur has two legs.

If you were to learn that Arthur had lost a leg in an accident, you would withdraw the conclusion. Yet, in logic it remains valid because no subsequent information can subtract from the set of conclusions that follow validly from any premises. Logic is monotonic: further premises can only add to the set of valid conclusions. Hence, it seems that everyday inference cannot be based on logic. One way out is to argue that the premise, "Persons have two legs," is simply false. But this stratagem gives up too much. It is useful to assume that people have two legs, and to take for granted the truth of many other similar assertions, because the valid deductions that they support usually yield true conclusions.

An alternative stratagem is to try to frame a *non-monotonic* logic that allows conclusions to be withdrawn in the light of subsequent information. A major proponent of artificial intelligence, Marvin Minsky (1975), has suggested the use of default values. The concept of person, for example, is represented with various variables, and the variable for number-of-legs has its value set by default to two, provided that there is no information to the contrary. Reiter (1980) has similarly introduced the notion of default rules of inference of the form:

If A, and it is consistent to infer B, then infer B.

Hence, given the proposition, Arthur is a person, one can infer that Arthur has two legs provided that this proposition cannot be disproved. There are several other systems of non-monotonic reasoning that have been developed within artificial intelligence. The trouble, as Reiter (1980) pointed out, is that they are systems for which no formal procedure can be guaranteed to determine the validity of an inference.

In fact, the withdrawal of a conclusion can occur at two distinct levels in daily life. At a low level, it occurs when reasoners make an assumption by default, and then subsequent evidence forces them to revise it. It also occurs, however, at a higher level, when an inference leads to a conclusion that is false in relation to some salient evidence or to a received body of knowledge. In this case, reasoners have to reconcile the discrepancy. They may be led to revise the inference itself, its premises, or their beliefs. The process of reconciliation is not a straightforward matter of deduction, but a search for a coherent explanation (see, e.g., Harman, 1986). How the reconciliation is carried out is largely unknown, but it operates at a higher-level than the ordinary processes of deduction and non-monotonic reasoning.

Content-Specific Rules and Production Systems

Minsky (1985) has written: "'Logic' is the word we use for certain ways to chain ideas. But I doubt that pure deductive logic plays much of a role in ordinary thinking." The progressive revelation of the difficulties of using formal deductive rules for machine reasoning has indeed led to some pessimism about the prospects of artificial intelligence based on formal logic (see McDermott, 1987). It has also seen a commensurate growth in direct attempts to model knowledge, often in the form of conditional rules with a specific content. Consider, for example, the following simple deduction:

> The plane is on the right of the refueler.
> The refueler is on the right of the hangar.
> ∴ The plane is on the right of the hangar.

In a system based on formal rules, the deduction cannot be made unless one adds an additional premise that makes explicit that *on the right of* is transitive:

> For any x, any y, any z, if x is on the right of y, and y is on the right of z, then x is on the right of z.

Such axioms are known as *meaning postulates* because they specify logical properties that depend on the meanings of predicates. An alternative possibility for a deductive computer program is to express the transitivity of *on the right of* directly in a rule of inference. The idea was originally developed in the programming language, PLANNER (Hewitt, 1972). The language allows the programmer to set up a large data base of facts, which might include the premises just presented:

(ON-RIGHT-OF PLANE REFUELER)
(ON-RIGHT-OF REFUELER HANGAR)

In addition, the programmer can add content-specific rules of inference, such as:

(CONSEQUENT (X Y Z) (ON-RIGHT-OF X Z)
  (GOAL (ON-RIGHT-OF X Y))
  (GOAL (ON-RIGHT-OF Y Z)))

This rule captures one consequence of the transitivity of the relation. It says, in effect, if you want to establish that x is on the right of z, then set up the subgoals of showing that x is on the right of y, and y is on the right of z. Someone using a program containing such a rule might inquire, "Is the plane on the right of the hangar?" The program first searches the data base to determine whether there is an assertion to that effect. Given a data base of just the two assertions above, this search will fail. At this point, the program attempts to match the enquiry:

(ON-RIGHT-OF PLANE HANGAR)

to the consequent of one of its rules of inference. Like the process of unification that I described earlier, the assertion will match the rule above and set the values of the relevant variables to specific entities; the program then attempts to satisfy the two subgoals:

(GOAL (ON-RIGHT-OF PLANE Y))
(GOAL (ON-RIGHT-OF Y HANGAR)))

These subgoals will be satisfied by the two assertions in the data base, where Y takes refueler as its value, and so the program can finally respond "yes" to the inquiry. Other enquiries may call for a longer chain of deductions; PLANNER also allows rules of inference that work forward from given data to new conclusions.

PLANNER has led to a variety of languages with similar capabilities. One particularly interesting format is a *production system* in which knowledge is encoded in a large body of conditional rules (*productions*) that are invoked by the specific contents of working memory. Production systems have been proposed as general models of cognitive architecture (Anderson, 1983; Newell, 1990), and as a way to represent human expertise in computer programs (Lindsay, Buchanan, Feigenbaum, & Lederberg, 1980). Although production systems are, in theory, as powerful as any other programming language, the logical powers of the standard programs written in such languages are markedly inferior to those of human beings (see the examples discussed further on in the section on multiple quantifiers).

PLANNER, production systems, and other such languages, allow general assertions to be expressed as content-specific rules of inference. Are such systems a syntactic or a semantic method of reasoning? The answer to this question will allow us to pin down the psychological distinction between syntax and semantics. Syntax concerns the form of expressions; semantics concerns the relation between expressions and situations in the world. The earlier rule for the transitivity of *on the right of* relates the form of one set of expressions to another, just as the rule for *modus ponens* relates the form of one set of expressions to another. Hence, despite their name, content-specific rules are not genuinely semantic: they do not relate expressions to the world, that is, they do not specify the truth conditions of assertions. The rules for *on the right of*, for example, have no machinery for relating particular arrangements of objects to the truth or falsity of the assertion, "The refueler is on the right of the plane." Such truth conditions are, as philosophers of language have argued, a necessary part of the meaning of assertions. Content-specific rules and formal rules of inference are, accordingly, syntactic, not semantic.

THE MENTAL MODEL THEORY OF DEDUCTION

Human Deductive Competence

Human reasoners exercise intelligence in ways that are conspicuously absent from machine reasoning. They are able to draw conclusions for themselves, and in so doing they abide by sensible constraints (Johnson-Laird, 1983). For instance, they do not normally throw semantic information away. Hence, given a premise, such as:

The plane is in front of the hangar.

they never spontaneously draw a final conclusion of the form:

The plane is in front of the hangar or it is raining, or both.

even though such a deduction is valid whatever the proposition that is added in the disjunction. They are parsimonious. They never, for example, draw a conclusion that merely conjoins all the premises, even though such a deduction is valid. They try to construct a conclusion that is not explicit in the premises. If no conclusion meets these constraints, then rather than draw some trivial, but valid, conclusion, they say, "There is no valid conclusion."

The human deductive mechanism is rapid, and seems to put as minimal a load as possible on the processing capacity of working memory. Because the heart of computational power is an ability to retain and exploit the results of intermediate computations, the mechanism is computationally weak, so it rapidly degrades with increasingly complex problems. A further sign of human intelligence, however, is the invention and use of systems of notation, including writing that can serve as a substitute for working memory. Writing enables human reasoners to cope with problems that demand more computational power. The metacognitive capacity to reflect on inferences and to develop notational systems to deal with them is a quintessential human competence.

A further mark of intelligence is the use of general knowledge in deductive inference. A reasoner's goal is to reach true, or at least plausible, conclusions rather than merely to make valid deductions. Knowledge can assist this process by providing pertinent information and a means for assessing the truth of conclusions. You are likely to judge that a conclusion is true if it corresponds to the state of affairs in the world or if it coheres with your other beliefs. Can beliefs directly affect the process of reasoning? The issue is highly controversial. If reasoning is based on formal rules, then the process itself cannot be affected by beliefs, but such effects are possible if reasoning is a semantic rather than a syntactic process. It is to this alternative view of the deductive mechanism that we now turn.

Mental Models

The first step in deduction is to establish a starting point, a set of observations founded, ultimately, on perception, verbal description, or imagination. Vision, as Marr (1982) has argued, calls for a series of representations that make high-level information progressively more explicit, culminating in a three-dimensional model of what things are where in the visual scene. Likewise, the comprehension of discourse yields an analogous model of the situation that is described (Johnson-Laird, 1983). Comprehension enables us to envisage situations that we have not yet perceived and perhaps never could perceive.

Much confusion has arisen over the idea of mental models because accounts differ from one theorist to another. The theory that my colleagues and I have developed is based on the following simple principles:

1. Each entity is represented by a corresponding token in a mental model.
2. The properties of entities are represented by the properties of their tokens.
3. Relations among entities are represented by relations among their tokens.

Thus, a model of the assertion, "The circle is on the right of the triangle" has the structure:

$\triangle$ $\bigcirc$

A model may be experienced as an image, but many models contain elements that cannot be visualized (e.g., the representation of negation). What matters is not the subjective experience, but the structure of the model. A model makes explicit those objects, properties, and relations, that are relevant to potential actions, that is, it makes them available to inference- and decision-making without the need for further processing. The structure of a model therefore corresponds to the structure of the situation, as humans conceive it, not to the linguistic structure of discourse. These structures differ from those of other proposed forms of representation, such as semantic networks (e.g., Quillian, 1968) or the representations used by formal rules (e.g., Braine et al., 1984). The difference becomes clear further on in the case of connectives, such as disjunction, and quantifiers, such as *all*.

The second stage in deduction is to formulate a putative conclusion. Because a model retains all the semantic information in the premises, a reasoner's main task is to draw a parsimonious conclusion that, if possible, expresses a relation that is not explicit in the premises.

The final stage in deduction is to test the validity of the putative conclusion. This process depends on establishing that there is no alternative model of the premises in which the conclusion is false. With simple deductions, human reasoners may be able to anticipate the alternative models, but with complex deductions they can seldom do so, and, as we shall see, they do not seem to be equipped with any systematic search procedure. To set the scene we first consider propositional reasoning, and then take up the problems of quantified reasoning.

Models and Propositional Reasoning

Propositional reasoning according to the model theory, consists in the construction and evaluation of mental models rather than the extraction and manipulation of logical forms. It is not a syntactic process, but a semantic process resembling the manipulation of truth tables, although individuals who have no training in logic are most unlikely to use truth tables: the number of rows in them increases exponentially with the number of elementary propositions contained in an argument and fails to correlate with the difficulty of deductions (Osherson, 1974–1976). The model theory, therefore, depends on an alternative semantic procedure proposed by Johnson-Laird and Byrne (1991). Reasoners using this procedure build models that represent as little as possible explicitly. As an illustration, consider again the premise:

If she was running after the train, then she was trying to catch it.

This conditional premise is initially represented by two models, one corresponding to the situation in which the antecedent is true, and the other corresponding to the situation in which it is false. (For the rest of this chapter, diagrams are used to represent mental models; when I depict the models of this conditional premise, I introduce the principles for interpreting the diagrams.)

The two models for the conditional are represented by the following diagram:

    [r]   c
     . . .

where each line corresponds to a model of an alternative possibility. The first line in the diagram denotes an explicit model of the situation in which the antecedent and consequent of the conditional are true: "r" denotes that part of the model representing the woman running after the train and "c" denotes that part of the model representing the woman trying to catch the train. The internal structure of such representations do not concern us until later when we encounter models of quantified assertions. The second line in the diagram, which consists of three dots, denotes a model that has no explicit content. According to the theory, reasoners do not initially think about this alternative situation, but they may subsequently replace the implicit model by one or more explicit models. The square brackets in the diagram of the first model indicate that the representation of the antecedent is somehow tagged to show that it has been exhaustively represented in relation to the consequent; that is, the antecedent, r, cannot occur elsewhere in the set of models. Hence, if the content of the implicit model were to be fleshed out explicitly, the resulting model, or models, could not contain any instances of r. By definition, if something is exhaustively represented, then no further instances of it can be added to a set of models. The consequent denoted by c, is not exhaustively represented, and so c could occur in an alternative to the first model.

Suppose that, in addition to the conditional premise, the further categorical assertion is made:

She was running after the train.

This premise eliminates the implicit model from the set of two representing the conditional: the premise asserts r, which occurs exhaustively in the first model, and so only this model remains:

[r]   c

It supports a novel conclusion, c, not stated in the premises:

∴. She was trying to catch the train.

and this conclusion is valid because there is no model of the premises that refutes it.

Now consider the premises for a *modus tollens* deduction:
If she was running after the train, then she was trying to catch it.
She was not trying to catch the train.

The first premise is again represented by the two models:

[r]   c
. . .

but the second premise eliminates the explicit model, which represents that she *was* trying to catch the train, and so only the implicit model survives. It seems that nothing follows from the premises, and, indeed, this response is by far the most frequent error that human reasoners make. Yet, some reasoners do succeed in making the *modus tollens* deduction. The theory explains their performance by postulating that they flesh out the implicit model of the conditional explicitly before they attempt to incorporate the information from the categorical premise. Because the consequent, c, is not exhaustively represented in the first model of the conditional, it may or may not occur in other models. If reasoners take the conditional premise to express a biconditional:

If, and only if, she runs after the train, then she is trying to catch it.

then they will flesh out the models in the following way:

$$r \qquad c$$
$$\neg r \qquad \neg c$$

where "$\neg$" represents negation (for a defense of such abstract elements, see the later section on the topic), and the exhaustion symbols are no longer necessary because all the models have been rendered completely explicit. If reasoners make the weaker conditional interpretation in which she can try to catch the train without running after it, then they will flesh out their models accordingly:

$$r \qquad c$$
$$\neg r \qquad c$$
$$\neg r \qquad \neg c$$

The second premise:

She was not trying to catch the train.

eliminates any model to the contrary, that is, any model containing c. Hence, regardless of which interpretation of the conditional is made, the result is a single model:

$$\neg r \qquad \neg c$$

and this model supports the conclusion:

∴ She was not running after the train.

Naturally, this deduction will be harder than *modus ponens* because the process of fleshing out calls for the construction of more than one explicit model. Readers who are interested in the details of the program for constructing propositional models should consult (Johnson-Laird & Byrne, 1991).

The bottleneck in inferential processing is the capacity of working memory, and so the model theory makes two principal predictions. First, the greater the number of explicit models needed for an inference, the harder the inference will be. Second, unlike formal theories, it also makes a prediction about the nature of erroneous conclusions: they should be conclusions that hold in only some models of the premises because subjects will sometimes fail to construct all the possible models. In short, the theory implies that people are deductive satisficers; if they come up with one conclusion that fits their available beliefs, they will tend not to search for others (with the potentially disastrous consequence of overlooking the correct conclusion).

Models and Quantificational Reasoning

The model theory extends in a natural way to deductions based on relations and quantifiers. The key, as always, is that reasoners must know the meanings of terms and use them to construct models of the situations described by the premises. There is nothing special about the logical connectives and quantifiers: their meanings must be grasped along with the meanings of nouns, verbs, adjectives, and other parts of speech. Given quantified premises, reasoners do not attempt to use formal rules of inference to manipulate logical forms, but rather model the situation described by the premises, formulate a novel conclusion, and search for alternative models that might refute this putative conclusion. The construction of models representing individuals, their properties, and relations, is a normal part of the process of comprehension, and the theory is, accordingly, closely related to other proposals for the representation of discourse (for a review, see Oakhill, Garnham, & Vonk, 1989).

The quantified assertion:

All the women were running for the train.

can be represented by a single model that represents some arbitrary number of women — say, three — all of whom were running for the train. A diagram of such a model has the following structure:

In this case, each token represents a separate individual. There are three women denoted by "w," and the brackets stand for the fact that the set of women has been exhaustively represented in the model. The "t" denotes a representation of the train, and the lines denote a representation of the relation, *running for*. The three dots represent the possibility of one or more other individuals (or entities) in the same situation. Because the women have been exhaustively represented, then implicitly, these other individuals are not women. The information from a second premise, such as:

Elizabeth was one of the women.

can be added to the model:

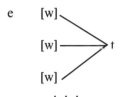

where "e" denotes the individual named Elizabeth. This model supports the conclusion:

∴ Elizabeth was running for the train.

This valid deduction is easy because it depends on only one explicit model. Other quantified deductions, as we shall see, call for the construction of more than one model.

RULES VERSUS MODELS

The previous sections have outlined the two main theoretical approaches to the psychology of deduction: syntactic theories based on rules of inference and semantic theories based on mental models. We now confront these two kinds of theory with the psychological evidence. Logicians distinguish three main branches of deduction: propositional deductions, which depend on connectives; relational deductions, which depend on relations, such as *on the right of, larger than, parent of;* and quantified deductions, which introduce in addition such quantifiers as *none, any,* and *some.* Psychologists have followed logic, and so we will consider experimental findings from these three domains. We start, however, with effects of content on human reasoning because prima facie they are inimical to any purely formal approach to deduction.

The Effects of Content on Human Reasoning

Wason's selection task demonstrates the potent effect of content on reasoning (see Wason, 1966, 1983). In the original version of the task, subjects are presented with four cards laid on a table: A, B, 2, 3. They know that these cards have been taken from a pack in which each card has a letter on one side and a number on the other side. They are given the following conditional rule:

If a card has an A on one side, then it has a 2 on the other side.

and they are asked to select just those cards which, if they were turned over, would enable them to determine whether the assertion is true or false. Nearly all subjects select either the A and the 2 card, or the A card alone. What is surprising is their failure to select the 3 card (corresponding to the negated consequent of the conditional) because if this card had an A on its other side, the rule would be plainly false.

The use of a more realistic content enables subjects to gain insight into the task (Johnson-Laird, P. Legrenzi, & M. S. Legrenzi, 1972; Wason & Shapiro, 1971). The effects are labile, but significantly more subjects select the card corresponding to the negated consequent with the following more realistic assertion:

If a person is drinking beer then the person must be over 18.

Subjects tend to choose the card representing a person drinking beer, and the card representing a person less than 18 years in age (Cheng & Holyoak, 1985; Griggs & Cox, 1982).

Formal theories cannot readily explain either the failure to select the negated consequent in the original version of the task or its correct selection with more realistic conditionals (see, e.g., Manktelow & Over, 1987; Wason & Johnson-Laird, 1972). The logical forms of the two sorts of conditional appear to be identical, and the card that negates the consequent ought to be selected whether subjects make a conditional or a biconditional interpretation. The only recourse for formalists is to claim that the selection task does not elicit deductive inferences (Rips, 1990), but if subjects do not reason in the selection task, then one is entitled to ask under what circumstances, if any, they do make deductions.

In fact, there is a natural explanation of the selection task in terms of the model theory of deductive reasoning. The theory makes three assumptions. First, reasoners consider only those cards that are explicitly represented in their models of the conditional assertion. This assumption applies *mutatis mutandis* to any form of deduction: one can reason only on the basis of what one has represented. Second, reasoners sensibly select only those cards from within the represented set that bear on the truth or falsity of the rule. Third, various factors including general knowledge, can lead reasoners to flesh out their models of the conditional more explicitly. The models of a conditional such as:

If there is an A on one side of a card, then there is a 2 on the other side.

can be represented by the following diagram:

    [A] | 2
        . . .

where the vertical barrier demarcates the two sides of the card. Hence, subjects consider only these two cards, and select either the A and the 2 cards, or the A card alone. They select the 2 card as a result of a bias toward verifying the rule; it cannot falsify the rule. Any manipulation that leads subjects to flesh out their models explicitly:

    A | 2
    ¬A | 2
    ¬A | ¬2

will lead to greater insight into the task. The subjects will now consider the card corresponding to the negated consequent and should therefore be more likely to select it. Among the manipulations that should lead to such a fleshing out of models is the use of a content that elicits a knowledge of the hitherto missing contingencies. This knowledge may be represented by content-specific rules (*pragmatic reasoning schemas*) as Cheng and Holyoak (1985) have proposed, but knowledge alone does not provide a full account of the phenomena. When the load on working memory is reduced by simplifying the conditional rule so that it refers only to a single object (e.g., "if there's a triangle then it is white"), the probability of fleshing out the models is enhanced, and indeed subjects have greater insight into the task (Oakhill & Johnson-Laird, 1985b; Wason and Green, 1984).

Beliefs and prejudices have long been said to influence deductive reasoning (Henle, 1962; Revlin & Leirer, 1978), but, according to formalists, they act as a bias on the initial interpretation of premises, or as a "censor" that throws out obviously false conclusions or that demands a check of the proof of them. They could not affect the process of deduction itself because formal rules are, by definition, blind to content. In contrast, according to the model theory, beliefs could influence the deductive process because reasoners should search harder for alternative models of the premises if an initial putative conclusion offends their beliefs.

Although many studies have been carried out on the effects of beliefs on reasoning, most of them have been methodologically flawed. Either they have taken no independent measure of the subjects' beliefs or they have presented conclusions for evaluation so that their plausibility might have been judged without any reasoning at all. Recent studies, however, have examined the influence of beliefs on conclusions that subjects draw for themselves (Oakhill & Johnson-Laird, 1985a; Oakhill, Johnson-Laird, & Garnham, 1989). These studies used materials in which an initial putative conclusion was either congruent or incongruent with subjects' beliefs, a manipulation that produced a striking effect on deductive performance. For instance, when subjects were given the premises:

All of the Frenchmen are wine drinkers.
Some of the wine drinkers are gourmets.

most of them (72%) drew the conclusion:

∴ Some of the Frenchmen are gourmets.

When they were given premises with the same logical form but a different content:

All of the Frenchmen are wine drinkers.
Some of the wine drinkers are Italians.

hardly any subjects (8%) drew the corresponding conclusion:

∴ Some of the Frenchmen are Italians.

The model theory predicted the difference on the following grounds. In the first case, subjects build a single initial model of the form:

```
[f]     w     g
[f]     w     g
[f]     w
        . . .
```

where "f" denotes a Frenchman, "w" denotes a wine drinker, and "g" denotes a gourmet. This model supports the conclusion:

∴ Some of the Frenchmen are gourmets.

Because this initial conclusion is congruent with the subjects' beliefs (as assessed by an independent panel from the same population), they do not search assiduously for an alternative model that might refute it.

In the second case, subjects build the same sort of model:

```
[f]    w    i
[f]    w    i
[f]    w
        . . .
```

where "i" denotes an Italian. This initial model supports the conclusion:

∴ Some of the Frenchmen are Italians.

but this conclusion is contrary to the subjects' beliefs (as assessed by the panel) and so they are more likely to search for an alternative model, such as:

```
[f]    w
[f]    w
[f]    w
       w    i
       w    i
        . . .
```

This model still represents the premises, but it refutes the conclusion, and so the subjects respond, "Nothing follows."

These and other studies (Evans, Barston, & Pollard, 1983; Markovits & Nantel, 1989) show that beliefs can have a direct influence on inferential processes, an hypothesis advanced by Heider (1958) (and rejected by others such as Nisbett & Ross, 1980), which has received independent support from studies of social reasoning (see Kunda, 1990). Formal theories cannot easily explain the phenomenon. They cannot refer to the believability of the initial putative conclusions, because these invalid conclusions do not occur in formal derivations from the premises. The model theory, however, predicts this phenomenon of deductive satisficing: if subjects reach a conclusion that fits their beliefs, they will tend not to search for others.

Propositional Reasoning

Formal theories have chiefly been proposed for propositional reasoning, and they have been assessed in three main studies of large batteries of deductions (Braine et al., 1984; Osherson, 1974–1976; Rips, 1983). In his pioneering study, Osherson investigated children's and adolescents' ability to evaluate various sorts of deduction. In order to account for his data, he made several assumptions motivated by previous findings. Because these assumptions can be accounted for by the model theory, I describe them rather than the data. One of Osherson's major assumptions is that it is easier to make deductions from conjunctions than from disjunctions. The difference undoubtedly exists, but it cannot be *explained* by formal theories. They can only stipulate that there is a difference in the availability or ease of use of the corresponding rules. The difference is predicted by the model theory, however, because a conjunction requires only one explicit model, whereas a disjunction requires at least two explicit models. Thus, the conjunction:

There is a circle and there is a triangle.

is represented by the model:

○   △

whereas the disjunction:

There is a circle or there is a triangle.

requires at least two alternative models:

○
    △

Osherson's second assumption is that *modus ponens* is easier than *modus tollens,* and we have already seen how the model theory accounts for this difference. His third assumption is that negative premises cause difficulty. Negation is a well-known cause of difficulty in comprehension. A double negation, such as:

It is false that there is not a triangle.

is harder to understand than the logically equivalent affirmative:

It is true that there is a triangle.

The model theory introduces an additional effect of negation: the number of models that negation yields. The negation of a conjunction:

It is not the case that there is both a circle and a triangle.

should be a particularly difficult premise, because it calls for three distinct
models:

○   ¬△
¬○   △
¬○   ¬△

I show, further on, that this prediction is corroborated by experimental
results.

In a different study of a battery of deductions (Rips, 1983), subjects
judged whether given conclusions followed from premises. The subjects'
overall performance was at a chance level , but half of the problems violated
one of the main constraints on everyday deduction that we discussed earlier:
the conclusions threw away semantic information from the premises. The
problems that maintained semantic information were correctly evaluated on
66% of occasions, whereas those that threw semantic information away
were evaluated on only 35% of occasions, a difference that was highly
significant. Other formalists have expressed a methodological worry about
the experiment. In commenting on the difficulty of certain deductions,
Braine et al. (1984) wrote, "So high a failure rate on transparent problems
suggests that the experiment often failed to engage the reasoning procedures
of subjects" (p. 360).

In Braine et al.'s own study, the subjects rated the difficulty of propositional deductions about letters on an imaginary blackboard. The data were
then used to assess parameters for the availability of the different formal
rules, which yielded a reasonable fit of the theory to the data. The premises
and the conclusions both varied unsystematically in their complexity, but
the model theory does make a global prediction (see Johnson-Laird, Byrne,
& Schaeken, 1992). All 61 of the direct deductions that the subjects
evaluated can be made without fleshing out the initial models of the
premises. We implemented the model theory in a computer program that
counted the number of explicit models that had to be constructed for each
problem. This number and the presence or absence of double-negative
premises correlated just as well (0.8) with the subjects' ratings as did Braine
et al.'s analysis in terms of the length of formal derivations. The model
theory also explains many aspects of the data without the need to estimate
parameters. For example, the theory predicts the following rank order of
difficulty of connectives in terms of the number of models that they require:

and	1 explicit model
if	1 explicit and 1 implicit model
or	2 explicit models
not both . . . and . . .	3 explicit models

The subjects' mean ratings of the difficulty of problems based on a simple categorical premise and a premise containing one of these connectives, significantly corroborated this prediction:

and   mean rating of 1.79
if   mean rating of 1.88
or   mean rating of 2.66
not both . . . and . . .   mean rating of 3.18

where a rating of 1 = *easiest,* and a rating of 9 = *hardest.*

In fact, the model theory explains all the robust phenomena of propositional reasoning. It also makes a number of novel predictions, including the rank order in the relative difficulty of connectives. One prediction is particularly important because it cannot be made by formal theories. According to the model theory, erroneous conclusions occur because reasoners construct and evaluate only some of the possible models of the premises. The content of erroneous conclusions should, therefore, correspond to a proper subset of the premise models. This prediction was confirmed in a study of so-called "double disjunctions" (Johnson-Laird et al., 1992). When subjects were given such premises as:

Linda is in Amsterdam or Cathy is in Palermo, but not both.
Cathy is in Quebec or Fiona is in Stockholm, but not both.

they often drew erroneous conclusions. Nearly all of these errors were conclusions that follow from some of the possible models of the premises. Thus, the premises support the models:

[a]   [s]
[a]   [q]
        [p]   [s]

where "a" denotes "Linda is in Amsterdam," "s" denotes "Fiona is in Stockholm," "q" denotes "Cathy is in Quebec," and "p" denotes "Cathy is in Palermo" (and she cannot be in both places). Concluding that:

Linda is in Amsterdam and Fiona is in Stockholm.

is erroneous, but it is supported by one of the possible models. In fact, the most frequent sort of error with double disjunctions is a conclusion that holds in only one model. This result cannot be easily explained by formal theories. Given premises of the form of those in the previous problem:

a or p, but not both
q or s, but not both

and the premise asserting that Cathy cannot be in two places at the same time:

if p then not q

there are no formal rules in Rips's (1983) theory or in Braine et al.'s (1984) theory that could yield the invalid conclusion:

a and s

Indeed, the rules cannot yield invalid conclusions in any systematic way. All that can go wrong is that either reasoners are unable to find a derivation or that they misapply a rule. Mistakes of this sort, however, cannot explain why the most frequent errors correspond to one model of the premises, or why nearly all the erroneous conclusions correspond to a proper subset of the models. Finally, this study confirmed the predicted difference between exclusive and inclusive disjunctions: exclusive disjunctions are easier because they yield fewer explicit models than inclusive disjunctions.

Relational Reasoning

Early studies of relational reasoning concentrated on three-term series problems, such as:

Arthur is taller than Bill.
Charles is shorter than Bill.
Who is tallest?

They could be solved by constructing a model (De Soto, London, & Handel, 1965) or by carrying out quasi-linguistic operations (Hunter, 1957). The resulting controversy revealed only one incontrovertible fact: the domain was not rich enough to determine how reasoners made such deductions. They are undoubtedly affected by linguistic aspects of the premises (see Clark, 1969), yet they could also be reasoning by constructing models (Huttenlocher, 1968). The controversy is easier to resolve by considering a more complex form of relational reasoning: two-dimensional spatial deductions.

Here is a simple problem that we have investigated (Byrne & Johnson-Laird, 1989):

The fork is on the right of the spoon.
The cup is on the left of the spoon.
The knife is in front of the cup.
The plate is in front of the fork.
What is the relation between the knife and the plate?

Previous studies had shown that subjects tend to imagine symmetric layouts with comparable distances between adjacent objects (see Ehrlich & Johnson-Laird, 1982; Mani & Johnson-Laird, 1982). The model theory accordingly predicts that reasoners should construct a symmetrical spatial model of the premises. We can illustrate the structure of such a model in a spatial diagram in which we will label the objects in their positions (as though one were looking at them on a table):

```
cup           spoon         fork
knife                       plate
```

This model supports the conclusion:

∴ The knife is on the left of the plate.

which no model of the premises refutes.
    A similar problem can be constructed by changing just one word in the second premise:

The fork is on the right of the spoon.
The cup is on the left of the fork.
The knife is in front of the cup.
The plate is in front of the fork.
What is the relation between the knife and the plate?

The model theory predicts that the same model as before can be con-structed:

```
cup           spoon         fork
knife                       plate
```

but the premises do not fix the relation between the spoon and the cup. Hence, the following model is equally good:

```
spoon         cup           fork
              knife         plate
```

Both models yield the same answer:

∴ The knife is on the left of the plate.

and so it remains correct. According to the model theory, this inference should be harder than the previous one because reasoners have to construct more than one model in order to make the right response for the right reason.

Theories based on formal rules call for postulates that specify the logical properties of relations. The following postulate, for instance, specifies that *on the right of* is a transitive relation:

For any x, any y, any z, if x is on the right of y, and y is on the right of z, then x is on the right of z.

Both Hagert (1984) and Ohlsson (1984) have proposed such formal rules for two-dimensional spatial deductions. It is easy to show that any formal theory should make the opposite predictions to those of the model theory. The premises of the one-model problem establish the explicit relations shown by the arrows in the following diagram:

```
cup   →   spoon   ←   fork
 ↑                     ↑
knife                 plate
```

Before the relation between the knife and plate can be inferred, it is, therefore, necessary to infer the relation between the cup and the fork. This inference calls for two steps: the conversion of the relation between the fork and the spoon, and then the transitive inference to the conclusion that the cup is on the left of the fork. In the case of the multiple-model problem, however, the following relations are established by the premises:

```
 ┌──────────────────────►
cup       spoon   ←   fork
 ↑                     ↑
knife                 plate
```

It is not necessary to infer the relation between the cup and the fork, because it is directly asserted in a premise. The length of the derivation will therefore be shorter, and so such problems should be easier than the one-model problems.

We carried out several experiments to investigate the relative difficulty of these problems, and their results were uniform (Byrne & Johnson-Laird,

1989). One-model problems were reliably easier than multiple-model problems. In one of our experiments, for example, there were 70% correct responses to the one-model problems, but only 46% correct to the multiple-model problems. Hence, the results corroborate the model theory but run counter to the formal theories.

Could the instruction to imagine the layouts have led the subjects to adopt a strategy otherwise alien to them? It is unlikely. Indeed, it is difficult to influence reasoning strategies by explicit instructions (e.g., Dickstein, 1978), and when researchers have manipulated the imageability of premises, they have failed to detect any significant effects on relational reasoning (Richardson, 1987). The critical feature of models is that their structure corresponds to that of situations, not that they should be experienced as images. Human reasoners seem to make spatial inferences by constructing models of the premises.

Reasoning With Quantifiers: Syllogisms

No one has proposed a comprehensive psychological theory of quantified reasoning based on formal rules, perhaps because the lengths of formal derivations in the predicate calculus fail to correlate with the difficulty of deductions. The model theory, however, was originally developed in order to explain inferences drawn from premises containing single quantifiers, that is, syllogisms (see Johnson-Laird, 1975). Some syllogisms are so difficult that hardly anyone can do them; others are so easy that even 9-year-old children spontaneously draw valid conclusions (Johnson-Laird, Oakhill, & Bull, 1986). Given the following premises, for example:

Some of the teachers are parents.
All of the parents are drivers.

nearly everyone concludes:

∴ Some of the teachers are drivers.

The model theory postulates that reasoners represent sets of individuals by constructing corresponding mental sets of a small, arbitrary number of tokens. Hence, according to a recent formulation (Johnson-Laird & Byrne, 1991), the first premise in the example elicits a single model representing a small, but arbitrary, number of teachers and parents. The following diagram represents the essentials of the model:

t   p
t   p
   . . .

Each line corresponds to a single individual: "t" represents a teacher, "p" represents a parent, so the first two lines correspond to individuals who are both teachers and parents. The three dots correspond to at least one other implicit individual, who may or may not exist. Neither the teachers nor the parents are exhaustively represented (as shown by the absence of square brackets). The information in the second premise can then be added to the model to yield:

```
t    [[p]    d]
t    [[p]    d]
     . . .
```

where "d" represents a driver. The model represents parents exhaustively with respect to drivers (i.e., further parents added to the model must also be drivers, but further drivers added to the model need not be parents).

A conclusion is generated by scanning the model to determine whether it supports any relation that is not stated in the premises. In this case, there is such a conclusion:.

∴ Some of the teachers are drivers

The conclusion cannot be drawn about *all* the teachers, because they are not exhaustively represented in the model. The model also supports the converse conclusion:

∴ Some of the drivers are teachers.

but we discovered in our earlier studies that there is a strong *figural bias*: subjects draw the first of these two conclusions more often than the second (Johnson-Laird & Steedman, 1978). In the final stage of reasoning, the conclusion is evaluated by checking whether it is falsified by some other model of the premises. No such model refutes the present conclusion, and so it is valid.

In general, a syllogism of the form:

Some of the A are B.
All of the B are C.

has the following *figure,* or arrangement of terms:

A - B
B - C

and subjects tend to draw conclusions of the form:

  A - C

The figural bias is probably a result of the order in which information is combined in working memory: conclusions are formulated in the same order in which the information is used to construct a model. Alternatively, the bias may reflect a pragmatic preference for making the subject of a premise into the subject of the conclusion (Wetherick & Gilhooly, 1990). This linguistic bias, however, fails to explain the progressive slowing of responses over the four figures of the syllogism, that is, the following arrangements of the terms in the premises:

A - B	B - A	A - B	B - A
B - C	C - B	C - B	B - C.

This phenomenon is accounted for by the *working memory hypothesis,* which postulates both the reordering of information in a premise and the re-ordering of the premises themselves in order to bring the two occurrences of the middle term into temporal contiguity (Johnson-Laird & Bara, 1984).

Deductions should be difficult according to the model theory, if they call for the construction of multiple models. Consider the following single premise:

Some of the teachers are not parents.

For individuals other than logicians, it has a model of the form:

```
t
t    [p]
     [p]
  . . .
```

where the set of parents is exhaustively represented. Readers familiar with scholastic logic will note that an exhaustive representation corresponds to a "distributed" term. This initial model supports the conclusion:

Some of the parents are not teachers.

The conclusion is invalid but many people commit the error (see Woodworth & Schlosberg, 1954). In fact, an alternative model of the premise:

```
t
t    [p]
t    [p]
  . . .
```

refutes the conclusion, so those subjects who can construct and evaluate both models will refrain from the fallacious inference.

Those syllogisms that are difficult also require multiple models. The following premises, for example:

All of the parents are teachers.
None of the parents is a driver.

yield the model:

```
[t     [p]]
[t     [p]]
              [d]
              [d]
     . . .
```

in which the set of parents is exhausted in relation to the set of teachers but not vice versa, and the set of drivers and parents are mutually exhausted with respect to one another. This model supports the invalid conclusion:

None of the teachers is a driver.

which is the most common error made with the premises. It is refuted by the following model:

```
[t     [p]]
[t     [p]]
 t            [d]
              [d]
     . . .
```

and the two models together support the conclusions:

Some of the teachers are not drivers.
Some of the drivers are not teachers.

The latter conclusion is, in turn, refuted by the model:

```
[t     [p]]
[t     [p]]
 t            [d]
 t            [d]
     . . .
```

Some subjects, at this point, are tempted to conclude that there is no valid conclusion. In fact, all three models support a conclusion that cannot be refuted:

∴ Some of the teachers (i.e., those who are parents) are not drivers.

This multiple-model problem, not surprisingly, is one of the hardest of syllogisms.

The evidence on syllogistic inference has been published elsewhere (see Johnson-Laird & Bara, 1984; Johnson-Laird et al., 1986; Johnson-Laird & Steedman, 1978). It shows that, for every subject whom we have ever tested, one-model problems are considerably easier than those that call for multiple models. The theory also accounts for the most common errors: as in the case of propositional reasoning, they are conclusions that correspond to some of the possible models of the premises, typically, just a single model.

This principle offers an alternative explanation for those errors that originally motivated the atmosphere effect described in the Prologue, and similar matching biases proposed by Wetherick and Gilhooly (1990) and M. Levine (personal communication, March, 1991). The atmosphere of the premises may have little or no effect on reasoning—the errors it predicts are nearly all predicted by the model theory—and where the model theory does not predict them, they do not occur (see Johnson-Laird & Byrne, 1989). In particular, all one-model syllogisms have correct responses that match the mood of at least one premise, but there are multiple-model problems where the correct response also matches the mood of at least one premise. If matching is the decisive factor then both sets of problems should be equally easy, but if number of models is the decisive factor, then the one-model problems should be easier than the multiple-model problems. In fact, the frequency of correct responses (from four independent experiments) were: 76% correct for the one-model problems, and 42% correct for the multiple-model problems. The difference was highly reliable (Mann-Whitney $U = 0.5$, $p < .01$). Matching cannot explain the difference; number of models appears to be the decisive factor (see Johnson-Laird & Byrne, 1991, for further arguments against atmosphere effects).

The model theory has been implemented in several computer programs. What drives the programs after the construction of the initial conclusions is the search for a falsifying model; in some cases, the construction of such a model may call for several separate operations to be carried out. The programs differ in the particular numbers of models that they construct for multiple-model problems; people may differ in a similar way.

The Evidence for Abstract Symbols in Models

One controversy among those who propose model theories is whether models contain tokens representing negation, exhaustiveness, and other abstract ideas. Some theorists argue that models represent only physical objects and their perceptible properties, and that abstract notions are handled outside the models themselves (see Inder, 1987; Levesque, 1986, for an analogous restriction in AI representations). Others argue that models can contain tokens representing abstract ideas (Newell, 1990; Polk & Newell, 1988). The issue has been addressed by evidence from experiments with the quantifier *only* (Johnson-Laird & Byrne, 1989).

When subjects are asked to consider a pair of assertions, such as:

All the participants are ticketholders.
Only the ticketholders are participants.

they grasp at once their similarity, but they do not immediately realize that the two assertions have identical truth conditions. One reason may be the order of the terms in the two assertions and, thus, the order in which their models are constructed. There is probably another reason, too. The model for "All the participants are ticketholders" has, according to the theory, the following initial structure:

[p]   t
[p]   t
 . . .

which contains explicit information only about participants and ticketholders. It can subsequently be fleshed out to represent the following situation:

  p   t
  p   t
 ¬p   t
 ¬p   ¬t

in which there is a nonparticipant who is a ticketholder, and a person who is neither a participant nor a ticketholder. The model represents all the sets exhaustively, so there is no need for square brackets.

In contrast, the assertion:
Only the ticketholders are participants.

conveys, at once, both that anyone who is not a ticketholder is not a participant and that participants are ticketholders:

```
    t        [p]
    t        [p]
 [ ¬ t]     ¬ p
      . . .
```

There could also be a ticketholder who is not a participant: What is asserted is that only the ticketholders are participants, not that all the ticketholders are participants. Hence, the model can be fleshed out to represent the following situation:

```
    t        p
    t        p
    t       ¬ p
   ¬ t      ¬ p
```

Apart from the order of the terms, this model is identical to the model for "All the participants are ticketholders."

The difference between the initial representations of the *all* and *only* assertions yields a testable prediction. An inference akin to *modus ponens*:

> All the participants are ticketholders.
> John is participant.
> ∴ John is a ticketholder.

should be relatively easy to carry out. The model of the premises:

```
   j     [p]    t
         [p]    t
          . . .
```

where "j" stands for John, immediately yields the conclusion that John is a ticketholder. An inference akin to *modus tollens*:

> All the participants are ticketholders.
> John is not a ticketholder.

should be more difficult, because a token for John cannot be added to the initial model. The model must first be fleshed out with information about people who are not ticketholders. Such an individual cannot be a participant because that set is already exhaustively represented:

```
[ p]      t
[ p]      t
¬ p     ¬ t
   . . .
```

Now, the token for John can be added to the model:

```
[ p]      t
[ p]      t
¬ p     ¬ t    j
   . . .
```

to yield the conclusion:

∴ John is not a participant.

When these two deductions are based on the assertion, "Only the ticketholders are participants," the theory predicts that there should no difference in difficulty between them: the initial model represents *both* the relevant sets (the ticketholders and the nonparticipants):

```
   t     [ p]
   t     [ p]
[ ¬ t]   ¬ p
[ ¬ t]   ¬ p
   . . .
```

and so the token representing John can be immediately added in order to make either inference. This prediction has been confirmed experimentally (Johnson-Laird & Byrne, 1989). Plainly, if negation were not directly represented in models, it would be difficult to account for the phenomena. Granted that people construct models in order to reason, their models do contain tokens representing abstract ideas. The significance of such tokens as "¬" depends on the procedures that relate assertions to models, and models to the world: negation calls for such a token in a model, and the token calls for negation in the formulation of a conclusion.

Reasoning With Multiply Quantified Relations

Some theorists believe that a quantified assertion, such as, "All the participants are ticketholders," is mentally represented by Euler circles (see, e.g., Erickson, 1974). Such a representation consists of two circles, one representing the set of participants and the other representing the ticketholders; the first circle is either included within the second or coextensive with it, representing the two possible relations consistent with the premise. Different arrangements of the circles can capture the meaning of the other forms of syllogistic premise. Euler circles, however, are not powerful enough to represent relations between two or more quantified arguments (Gardner, 1982). In contrast, models based on individual tokens naturally extend to cope with multiple quantifiers, as two examples will illustrate. Consider, first, the following:

None of the Avon letters is in the same place as any of the Bury letters.
All of the Bury letters are in the same place as all of the Caton letters.

These premises yield the following sort of model, where the vertical barriers demarcate separate places, and the numbers of tokens, as before, are arbitrary:

| a a a | b b b c c c |

The "a's" denote Avon letters, the "b's" denote Bury letters, and the "c's" denote Caton letters. This model supports a novel conclusion:

∴ None of the Avon letters is in the same place as any of the Caton letters.

No alternative model of the premises refutes this conclusion, so it is valid. The theory predicts that the deduction should be easy because it is based on only one model, and the prediction has been corroborated experimentally: 71% of the subjects in a recent experiment spontaneously drew this conclusion, or linguistic variants of it (Johnson-Laird, Byrne, & Tabossi, 1989).

The second example is superficially similar to the first:

None of the Avon letters is in the same place as any of the Bury letters.
All of the Bury letters are in the same place as some of the Caton letters.

These premises yield the following sort of initial model:

| a a a | b b b c c | c c |

which also supports the conclusion:

None of the Avon letters is in the same place as any of the Caton letters.

This conclusion was the most frequent error, and it was drawn by 38% of the subjects. It is invalid because it can be refuted by an alternative model of the premises:

| a a a c c | b b b c c |

The two models together support the conclusion:

∴ Some of the Caton letters are not in the same place as any of the Avon letters.

or, equivalently:

∴ None of the Avon letters is in the same place as *some* of the Caton letters.

or the slightly weaker conclusion (in one of its interpretations):

∴ None of the Avon letters is in the same place as all of the Caton letters.

No models refute these conclusions, which are, therefore, valid. The theory predicts that this problem should be more difficult because it is necessary to construct multiple models. The results corroborated the prediction: Only 17% of subjects drew valid conclusions.

Table 1 presents a formal derivation in the predicate calculus. It shows how to derive the conclusion for the one-model example:

None of the Avon letters is in the same place as any of the Bury letters.
All of the Bury letters are in the same place as all of the Caton letters.
∴ None of the Avon letters is in the same place as any of the Caton letters.

It is necessary to represent the logical form of the premises in the predicate calculus:

1. $(\forall A)(\forall B) \neg (ASB)$
2. $(\forall B)(\forall C)(BSC)$

where "∀" denotes the universal quantifier, *any,* "¬" denotes negation, "S" denotes *in the same place as,* and the variables A, B, and C, are assumed to range over the relevant sets of letters: Avon, Bury, and Caton. The derivation depends on the fact that *in the same place as* is a transitive relation:

TABLE 1

A Formal Derivation in the Predicate Calculus. For Simplicity, I Have
Restricted Quantifiers to Particular Sorts of Sets.

The premises can be symbolized as:

1.	$(\forall A)(\forall B) \neg (ASB)$	(none of the A is in the same place as any of the B)
2.	$(\forall B)(\forall C)(BSC)$	(all of the B are in the same place as all of the C)
3.	$(\forall X)(\forall Y)(\forall Z)(XSY\ \&\ YSZ \rightarrow XSZ)$	
		(transitivity of "in the same place as")
4.	$(\forall X)(\forall Y)(XSY \rightarrow YSX)$	(symmetry of "in the same place as")

Stage 1: Instantiation of quantifiers

5.	$(\forall B) \neg (aSB)$	(universal instantiation of A in 1)
6.	$\neg (aSb)$	(universal instantiation of B in 5)
7.	$(\forall C)(bSC)$	(universal instantiation of B in 2)
8.	(bSc)	(universal instantiation of C in 7)
9–11.	$(aSc\ \&\ cSb) \rightarrow aSb$	(universal instantiations of X, Y, and Z in 3)
12,13.	$(bSc) \rightarrow (cSb)$	(universal instantiations of X and Y in 4)

Stage 2: Propositional reasoning

14.	$\neg (aSc\ \&\ cSb)$	(*modus tollens* from 6 and 11)
15.	$\neg (aSc)$ or $\neg (cSb)$	(de Morgan's law from 14)
16.	(cSb)	(*modus ponens* from 8 and 13)
17.	$\neg (aSc)$	(disjunctive rule from 15 and 16)

Stage 3: Re-introduction of quantifiers

18.	$(\forall C) \neg (aSC)$	(universal generalization of c in 17)
19.	$(\forall A)(\forall C) \neg (ASC)$	(universal generalization of a in 18)

The conclusion corresponds to:

∴ None of the A is in the same place as any of the C.

> If x is in the same place as y, and y is in the same place as z, then x is in
> the same place as z.

and that it is a symmetric relation:

> If x is in the same place as y, then y is in the same place as x.

Corresponding postulates are accordingly included in the statement of the
premises in Table 1.

The first stage in the proof is to eliminate the quantifiers. The calculus
has a rule of *universal instantiation* that says, in effect, if some property or
relation applies to every member of a set, then the quantifier can be
replaced by the name of any individual in that set. The particular choices of
instantiations of the postulates for symmetry and transitivity are not
obvious, but they are crucial for the derivation (see lines 9 to 13 in Table 1).
There are many possible instantiations of any set of quantified premises: as
the number of quantified terms increases, there is a combinatorial explosion

of possibilities. The aim of unification and the resolution rule of inference, which I described earlier, is to find the most fruitful instantiations.

The second stage in the proof is to derive a conclusion about the instantiated individuals using the formal rules for the sentential connectives. These rules can, of course, be framed in the way that psychologists have advocated for propositional reasoning (e.g., Braine, 1978; Rips, 1983).

The final stage in the proof is to restore appropriate quantifiers where necessary. When the so-called existential quantifier, *some,* is instantiated, then care must be taken not to name an individual that already occurs in the proof. When this individual is replaced by a quantifier in the final stage, then clearly the quantifier must be an existential.

Perhaps surprisingly, the proof for the multiple-model problem is almost identical to the one in Table 1. It has the same number of steps and differs at only two points. Because the second quantifier in the second premise is the existential quantifier, *some,* rather than the universal quantifier, *all,* an existential quantifier must be instantiated in line 8 of the proof and subsequently restored in the final line of the proof.

Any psychological theory based on formal rules for multiple quantifiers would have to surmount three severe difficulties. First, as we have seen, logic allows an infinite number of different valid conclusions to be derived from any set of premises, and does not determine which particular conclusion should be drawn. Human reasoners spontaneously tend to draw semantically strong conclusions, at least for one-model problems. The model theory readily accounts for this phenomenon: Reasoners do not throw semantic information away, because it is embodied in their models of the premises. The use of formal rules to search for a derivation of a *given* conclusion is hard enough, but to search for an unknown but semantically strong conclusion is still harder. There is no obvious way to guide the search so that it will automatically lead to such a conclusion. Theorists can constrain the rules for connectives so that they do not throw semantic information away, but the key to drawing the conclusion to the one-model problem in Table 1 is to make the right instantiations of the postulates for symmetry and transitivity. No a priori method exists for ensuring that these instantiations are made, and a method that tries out all possible instantiations seems a highly implausible maneuver for a deduction that takes human beings only a few seconds.

The second difficulty for a formal rule theory concerns the lengths of derivations and the ease of use of different rules. Formalists argue that the difficulty of a deduction depends on how many steps its derivation takes and on how hard it is to use the requisite rules. Yet, the one-model problem has a derivation that is identical in length to the derivation for the multiple-model problem. Because the multiple-model problem discussed earlier contained an existential quantifier, one might wonder whether this quantifier causes some special difficulty, but no such difficulty arises when an existential occurs in a one-model problem, such as:

Some of the Avon letters are in the same place as all of the Bury letters.
All of the Bury letters are in the same place as some of the Caton letters.

Subjects readily conclude:

∴ Some of the Avon letters are in the same place as some of the Caton letters.

One potential confounding, Greene (in press) claimed, is that the conclusions of the multiple-model problems are all of the form:

None of the X is in the same place as *some* of the Y.

and that sentences of this form are difficult to generate. However, other forms of conclusion for the multiple-model problems are both possible and generated by subjects. Assertions of the form:

Some of the Y are not in the same place as any of the X.

are equally valid, and there is no evidence to suggest that they are difficult to generate. Moreover, even if all the possible conclusions to multiple-model problems were difficult to generate, this factor alone could not account for the results. In particular, it would provide no explanation for the errors that subjects make.

The third difficulty for a formal rule theory is indeed to explain the systematic errors that occur with quantified deductions. This problem is best illustrated by the multiple-model example:

None of the Avon letters is in the same place as any of the Bury letters.
All of the Bury letters are in the same place as some of the Caton letters.

Some subjects draw the erroneous conclusion:

None of the Avon letters is in the same place as any of the Caton letters.

which suggests that they have constructed only the model:

| a a a | b b b c c | c c |

Other subjects make an error that seems very odd at first. They conclude:

All of the Avon letters are in the same place as some of the Caton letters.

In fact, this conclusion is precisely what one would expect from individuals who have considered only the model:

| a a a c c | b b b c c |

Some subjects modify this conclusion with a modal auxiliary:

All of the Avon letters *could* be in the same place as some of the Caton letters.

A modal conclusion is valid and informative provided that it holds in just some of the possible models of the premises. The theory therefore predicts that modal conclusions should be drawn more often with multiple-model problems than with one-model problems. The results confirm the prediction. In general, only 2% of conclusions to one-model problems were modal, whereas 20% of conclusions to multiple-model problems were modal. Once again, it is difficult to see how either the errors or the modal conclusions could occur in formal derivations. No obvious mechanism would yield errors that happen to correspond to just one model of the premises. Likewise, although formal modal calculi could be appropriated by psychologists, such accounts would still need to explain why modal conclusions happen to occur more often with multiple-model problems than with one-model problems. Until a formal theory is forthcoming that meets all of these difficulties, it seems safe to conclude that mental models offer the best available explanation of reasoning with quantifiers.

SOME MORALS FOR MACHINES

The model theory has implications for the design of machines for deduction. It suggests a new way in which to integrate knowledge, deduction, and non-monotonic reasoning, and a new way for programs to formulate their own conclusions. This section will consider these topics in turn, beginning with the integration of knowledge into reasoning processes.

Knowledge and Deduction

When people reason, they automatically rely on their general knowledge; when machines reason, their lack of knowledge is often a stumbling block. Consider, for example, the following problem:

Three children are standing in a line.
At least one of them is a girl, and at least one of them is a boy.
Is a girl standing next to a boy?

Problems of this sort defeat the standard theorem-proving apparatus embodied in PROLOG (R. Brachman, personal communication, March 1991), yet intelligent adults readily solve them. They imagine the children standing in line. Either the girl is standing next to the boy:

G   B   ?

or the third child of unknown gender intervenes:

G   ?   B

It is obvious from general knowledge that the third child is either a girl:

G   G   B

or a boy:

G   B   B

In either case, a girl is standing next to a boy. Models, as this problem shows, are a natural method of representation that can take into account any general knowledge that provides the values of unknowns.

When people reason, they automatically make non-monotonic inferences; that is, new information can lead them to withdraw an earlier conclusion. The attempts to accommodate non-monotonic reasoning within systems based on formal rules, as I mentioned earlier, have not been entirely successful. For the model theory, however, a combination of deductive and non-monotonic processes is essential if the theory is to cope with the indeterminacy of discourse (Johnson-Laird, 1983). Thus, any description of a situation is consistent with many alternative states of affairs. For instance, the assertion:

The desk is next to the table.

is satisfied by infinitely many different arrangements of the furniture. No one can envisage all of these possibilities, and so the model theory postulates that people make arbitrary assumptions in order to construct a model. One simple model is easily accommodated within working memory, but unfortunately it may not be the right model; that is, it may not match the situation under description. How, then, can one model stand in for any of the possible situations that might be correct? The answer is that the model can be modified to take into account subsequent information. Such modifications are allowed to change any component of the model that was assumed either arbitrarily or by default. The final model may still not correspond to the actual situation, but if the discrepancy matters, then, in principle it can be corrected by further assertions. Fortunately, everyday discourse is finite in length, so only a finite number of corrections will need to be made.

The way in which deduction and non-monotonic reasoning are integrated is illustrated by a program for spatial inference. Given the following premises:

The circle is on the right of the triangle.
The cross is on the left of the circle.

the procedure for constructing models interprets the first premise:

$\triangle$ $\bigcirc$

The second premise does not establish the relation between the cross and the triangle: the only constraint is that both are on the left of the circle. Hence, the program selects whichever relation is more convenient. In effect, it makes an arbitrary assumption about the relation between the two items:

$+$ $\triangle$ $\bigcirc$

Such assumptions keep the number of models to a minimum. If the program attempted to construct all possible models, it would soon exhaust its memory because the possibilities increase exponentially. If subsequent premises assert or imply that the cross is on the right of the triangle, then the model can be altered to take this information into account. The program progressively revises its models seeking to accommodate each new assertion. Default assumptions can be treated in the same way. The meaning of the word *triangle,* for example, could specify an equilateral triangle by default. If subsequent information conflicts with this assumption, the shape of the triangle can be revised.

Deduction depends on searching for alternative models of the premises that falsify a putative conclusion, because if the conclusion is true in all possible models of the premises, then it follows validly from them. The conclusion may have been true merely by chance or by default in the initial model, in which case there is a model that falsifies it. The key principle in these searches is, therefore, that the program is at liberty to undo both arbitrary and default assumptions. The same freedom is exploited in non-monotonic reasoning. If a premise turns out to be false in the current model, then a search is made for an alternative model of the previous premises that renders it true. If there is such a model, then the premise was false merely by chance or by default. The new model accommodates it by modifying the arbitrary or default assumption, and in this way makes a non-monotonic inference. If there is no model that renders the premise true, then it is genuinely inconsistent with the previous premises.

Reasoning by model is efficient. Programs can construct the minimum number of models and often represent discourse by only a single model. This efficiency is possible because the model can be changed, if necessary, to accept any new information that is consistent with the previous premises. The model serves as a representative sample from the set of possible models, but only a finite number of models needs to be considered because everyday discourse leads, at most, to only a finite number of revisions. Non-monotonic reasoning is, thus, essential for deductive reasoning by model: The two processes complement one another, and both depend on the search for alternative models.

Propositional Models and the Formulation of Conclusions

A mark of human intelligence, as I argued earlier, is the capacity to draw conclusions, but if infinitely many conclusions follow validly from any set of premises, then which conclusion should an intelligent program draw? Human reasoners tend to maintain the semantic information in the premises. They may not describe all the information in their models, but they do not throw information away by adding disjunctive alternatives. They try to re-express the information parsimoniously, although they fall into error if the number of models to be kept in mind increases too much. Nevertheless, the goal of parsimony provides a rational solution to the problem of which conclusion a deductive program should draw: It should express all the information in the premises as succinctly as possible.

In the propositional calculus, the task of finding a parsimonious re-expression of premises is equivalent to simplifying an electrical circuit made up of Boolean switches, which work as *not, and, or,* and other such units. The task is computationally expensive and becomes intractable as the size of the circuit increases (see Cook, 1971). The standard procedure is the *prime implicant* method (McCluskey, 1956; Quine, 1955), but it uses only *not, and,* and *or,* so it is not guaranteed to find the best simplifications. The model theory, however, has led to a. general propositional reasoning program that is an exercise in artificial intelligence (see Johnson-Laird, 1990). It copes with any deduction in the propositional calculus, although obviously the task becomes intractable when the size of a problem exceeds the computer's processing capacity. It can carry out all those deductions mentioned earlier that cause difficulty for natural deduction systems (Pelletier, 1986). It evaluates each premise to see whether it follows from the previous premises, or entails them; it also draws conclusions that express the information in the premises as parsimoniously as possible. Table 2 presents three typical examples of its performance.

The program constructs fully explicit models for the set of premises. Thus, for example, it interprets the premise:

If there is a circle and there is a triangle then there is an asterisk.

TABLE 2

Three typical examples of the outputs from the program for propositional reasoning. The program does not use brackets, but commas, which call for the interpretation of the next connective and its arguments: e.g., if a then, b and c, is equivalent to: (if a then (b and c)). Without the comma, the expression would be equivalent to: ((if a then b) and c)

1. *Input*
    a or b
    if a then c
    if b then d
    c or d
   Output
   This premise follows from those that preceded it: c or d.
   The premises are equivalent to:
      if a then c and, , if b then d and, a or b.
2. *Input*
    w or, if p then i
    if i then, c or s
    if s then u
    not c and not u
    not w.
   Output
   This premise follows from those that preceded it: not w.
   The premises are equivalent to:
      not w and, not p and, not i and, not c and, not s and not u.
3. *Input*
    if a then if b then c
    not d or a, and b
    if d then c
   Output
   This premise follows from those that preceded it: if d then c.
   The premises are equivalent to:
      b and, , if d then a and, if a then c.

by constructing the following set of models:

$$
\begin{array}{ccc}
\bigcirc & \triangle & * \\
\bigcirc & \neg\triangle & * \\
\neg\bigcirc & \triangle & * \\
\neg\bigcirc & \neg\triangle & * \\
\bigcirc & \neg\triangle & \neg* \\
\neg\bigcirc & \triangle & \neg* \\
\neg\bigcirc & \neg\triangle & \neg*
\end{array}
$$

The models are constructed "compositionally"; that is, as the program parses a premise, it uses semantic rules, which are matched one-to-one with the syntactic rules, to build the models. The meaning of the connective, *and*, is a function that takes two sets of models and constructs all their combinations apart from those that would be inconsistent with one another. Given the following two sets of models, for example:

$$
\begin{array}{ccc}
\bigcirc & \triangle & \neg* \\
\neg\bigcirc & \triangle & *
\end{array}
\qquad\qquad
\begin{array}{ccc}
\triangle & * & \Diamond \\
\triangle & \neg* & \Diamond
\end{array}
$$

it combines each model in the first set with each model in the second set, dropping those models that would contain an atom and its negation. It also ensures that there is only one occurrence of each atom, or its negation, in each of the final models:

$$
\begin{array}{cccc}
\bigcirc & \triangle & \neg* & \Diamond \\
\neg\bigcirc & \triangle & * & \Diamond
\end{array}
$$

The meaning of *not* is a function that returns the complement of a set of models. Thus, the negation of:

$$
\begin{array}{cc}
\bigcirc & \neg\triangle
\end{array}
$$

is:

$$
\begin{array}{cc}
\bigcirc & \triangle \\
\neg\bigcirc & \triangle \\
\neg\bigcirc & \neg\triangle
\end{array}
$$

The meanings of the other connectives are defined in terms of the meanings of *and* and *not*. The high-level function controlling the building of models loops through the list of premises, using the function for *and* to combine the models for each new premise with the existing models and checking to see whether one set entails the other. Because the syntactic and semantic rules are entirely general, the premises can be of any arbitrary degree of complexity.

A deduction is valid if the set of models for the premises is a subset of the conclusion models. For example, a deduction of the form:

If there is a circle then there is a triangle.
There is a circle.
∴ There is a circle and there is a triangle.

is valid because the premises yield a model:

○   △

that is a subset of the conclusion models:

○   △.

In this case, the two sets of models are identical. The premise models can also be a subset in another sense: it is not necessary for each element in the premise models to occur in the conclusion models. Hence, the conclusion:

∴ There is a triangle.

is also a valid deduction from the premises presented. Unlike a formal proof based on rules of inference, this method of reasoning does not depend on a search for a derivation: a simple check of the premise and conclusion models suffices to establish whether or not a deduction is valid.

Quantifiers and a Model-Based Programming Language

Can models be used for quantified deductions? The evidence certainly suggests that people reason in this way, but the question at stake is whether general deductive programs could be based on models. There are two immediate problems. First, the predicate calculus allows expressions that are true of infinite sets, but false of any finite set, for example,

For any number x, there is some number y, such that $y > x$.

A model can represent this assertion procedurally, by using a dynamic model that, given any number x, generates another, larger, number, y. Second, mental models depend on the truth conditions of assertions and thus on the contribution to such conditions made by each word in the language. This demand calls for a semantic analysis of the language, an analysis that, at present, is a long way from being realized by any semantic theory. It is possible, however, to finesse both of these difficulties, and to develop deductive procedures for quantifiers that are based on models.

The most general method applies both where sets may be infinite and where the semantics of the domain are not sufficiently understood for the construction of complete models. Like an orthodox theorem-prover, this method calls for the relevant logical properties of relations to be spelled out in meaning postulates, and for the instantiation of quantifiers. Consider, for example, the following premises (cf. Table 1):

1. $(\forall A)(\forall B) \neg(ARB)$ (none of the A is in relation, R, to any of the B)
2. $(\forall B)(\forall C)(BRC)$ (all of the B are in relation, R, to all of the C)
3. $(\forall X)(\forall Y)(XRY \longrightarrow YRX)$ (symmetry of relation, R)
4. $(\forall X)(\forall Y)(\forall Z)(XRY \ \& \ YRZ \longrightarrow XRZ)$ (transitivity of relation, R)

The first step, as in an orthodox theorem-prover, is to instantiate the quantified variables, that is, to replace them by hypothetical individuals (see the earlier discussion of reasoning with multiply quantified relations). The appropriate instantiations yield:

5. $\neg(aRb)$ (universal instantiations of 1)
6. (bRc) (universal instantiations of 2)
7. $(bRc) \longrightarrow (cRb)$ (universal instantiations of 3)
8. $(aRc \ \& \ cRb) \longrightarrow (aRb)$ (universal instantiations of 4)

The process of inference then proceeds, not by a search for a derivation using formal rules for the connectives, but by the construction of the corresponding models in which the relation, R, is left unanalyzed. The program, which was described in the previous section, interprets premises 5 and 6 and constructs the model:

$\neg(aRb)$ (bRc)

which represents the situation in which a is not related by R to b, and b is related by R to c. In fact, the model might take the following form, in which there is no duplication of tokens standing for the same individuals:

a $\neg$R b R c

It would then resemble the spatial models that we encountered earlier. The interpretation of premise 7 yields three models:

    (bRc)   (cRb)
    ¬(bRc)   (cRb)
    ¬(bRc)   ¬(cRb)

which, in combination with the model of the previous premises yields a single model:

    ¬(aRb)   (bRc)   (cRb).

Finally, the combination of this model with the models for premise 8 yields the model:

    ¬(aRb)   (bRc)   (cRb)   ¬(aRc).

The fourth item in this model is a relation that is not among the premises, and the restoration of universal quantifiers within it yields the conclusion:

    ∴ None of the A is in relation, R, to any of the C.

Although this method of deduction still requires a search for the appropriate instantiation of the premises, it has advantages over the use of formal rules for the connectives: (a) It does not call for a search for a derivation; the construction of models depends on a simple deterministic procedure; and (b) it automatically ensures that the semantically strongest conclusion will be forthcoming for each instantiation; an inappropriate instantiation merely fails to yield a set of models supporting a novel relation. For example, if the postulate for transitivity is instantiated as follows:

    (aRb & bRc) —> (aRc)

then the premises yield the following set of models:

    ¬(aRb)   (bRc)   (cRb)   (aRc)
    ¬(aRb)   (bRc)   (cRb)   ¬(aRc)

in which there is no determinate relation between a and c.

　　In domains with a well-understood semantics, it is possible to capture the meanings of relations in a way that enables complete models to be constructed. For example, in the spatial reasoning program that I described earlier, the semantics of each spatial relation ensures that objects are added to the array in appropriate places. Thus, a premise of the form, "The circle is on the left of the triangle," yields an array:

○   △

or adds whichever object is needed to satisfy the relation. If both objects are already in an array, the program verifies the relation. If it is true, then it is tested for validity; if it is false, then it is tested for a non-monotonic inference. Given an analysis of the truth conditions of assertions, that is, how they relate to models, then it is no longer necessary to specify the logical properties of a relation, such as its transitivity, asymmetry, and so on. These properties are emergent from the use of the relation's meaning in constructing models.

We have so far seen how to use models for connectives and relations, but the procedure for quantifiers still relies on instantiation, the replacement of quantified variables by hypothetical individuals. The complete use of models would abandon instantiation in favor of the direct representation of sets by individual tokens in models. A programming language based on this procedure corresponds to the full implementation of the psychological theory. It can be used only for the problems of daily life in which reasoners need to construct only a finite number of alternative models.

Machines and Meaning

The attentive reader will have noticed that, in describing the machine procedures for deduction, I have referred to semantic procedures and to the construction of models. Computer programs, however, are not truly semantic, because the symbols they manipulate have, as yet, no reference to the world, other than in the mind of the programmer. There is a twist in the tail of this argument. Defenders of formal rules often argue that the model theory is, at root, a syntactic one: the processes of constructing models, they say, call for formal rules of inference. Furthermore, they point to the computer programs implementing the model theory as a proof of their claim, yet the claim denies the crucial distinction that logicians draw between proof theory and model theory (see the earlier section on logic, form, and validity). If models could not be constructed and evaluated without relying on formal rules, then there would be no distinction between proof theory and model theory. Theorems, such as the proof of the completeness of the predicate calculus, that establish relations between these two domains would be vacuous.

The real moral of the computer programs is straightforward. Human reasoners understand the meaning of expressions. One day machines may have sufficiently rich connections with the world to do so, too, but meanwhile programs merely *simulate* semantics. The operation of the programs simulating the model theory, however, is quite different from any formalist theory. For instance, the models that a program constructs for "There is a circle or there is a triangle, or both":

○   △

○   ¬△

¬○   △

are isomorphic to a translation of the premise into *disjunctive normal form* (DNF):

There is a circle and there is a triangle, or
there is circle and there is not a triangle, or
there is not a circle and there is a triangle.

A corresponding formal theory would have to construct such translations, combine them, and evaluate them. Its rules would be quite remote from *modus ponens* and the other rules postulated by formalists as psychologically real. Indeed, as we have seen, the empirical consequences of such a theory would also be markedly different. Could human reasoners use DNFs, and formal rules for manipulating them? It is unlikely because human beings do understand the meanings of expressions. This process cannot consist in recovering a disjunctive normal form: DNF is merely another linguistic expression, which stands in need of semantic interpretation. Comprehension consists in the construction of models, which can be related to the world; deduction depends on a search for alternative models.

CONCLUSIONS

There are three fundamental differences between mental models and representations of logical form. First, models are semantic, whereas logical forms are syntactic. One uniform process of inference occurs using models: the construction of models, the formulation of conclusions, and the search for alternative models. Hence, all that is necessary in extending the theory to a new quantifier or connective is to specify its meaning. In the case of a formal theory, however, it is necessary to specify the appropriate rules of inference for the new term, and these rules will lead to new forms of derivation in proofs. Second, models contain no variables: everything is instantiated by a token or set of tokens during the process of interpretation, whereas logical forms are instantiated by hypothetical individuals during the course of deduction. Third, models are structures that integrate the information in premises: a referent is represented only once, and the relations between it and others are directly mirrored by relations in the model, whereas logical forms mirror the structure of discourse, so the same individual may be instantiated several times.

The differences between the two theories lead to different empirical predictions about the psychology of deductive reasoning. As this chapter has shown, the model theory has been experimentally corroborated in all the main areas of deduction: propositional reasoning, relational reasoning, and quantified reasoning. In each domain, the theory predicts the relative difficulty of different deductions and also explains the systematic nature of erroneous conclusions: human reasoners are satisficers (Simon, 1982). They tend to draw conclusions that hold for only some of the models of the premises — typically, just one of these models. The theory also accounts for the particular valid conclusions that subjects draw. They tend not to throw semantic information away because it is embodied in their models of the premises.

When these principles are used in machines for deduction, they confer certain advantages on the resulting system: it integrates deductive and non-monotonic reasoning; it replaces the search for derivations based on rules by a simple process of checking models. Models can be modified in the light of subsequent information that calls for the undoing of arbitrary assumptions or those made by default, and everyday reasoning calls for only a finite number of such modifications.

Skeptics sometimes view the model theory as merely an alternative formal theory, one that happens to give a better account of the psychological phenomena. Yet, human beings do represent the meanings of expressions, and the evidence suggests that they use these representations — in the form of models — in order to reason. To argue that semantic processes are merely syntactic is to commit the "formalist" fallacy that meaning can be reduced to form. Gödel's proof of the incompleteness of arithmetic, which I described earlier, should have dispelled this fallacy once and for all.

A deeper skepticism goes one step further and denies the significance of deduction in daily life. According to this claim, deduction is the prerogative of mathematicians and logicians. It seldom, if ever, occurs in everyday thought. This claim is exaggerated. The railway porter who saw Wittgenstein's colleague running after the train provides us with a typical case of everyday deduction. The real importance of deduction, however, is demonstrated by deductive failures. The engineers in charge at the Chernobyl power plant, for example, persisted in trying to carry out the experiment that led to the disaster even when it was easy to infer that it was impossible to do so because the turbine was rotating too slowly for the test to be conducted (see Medvedev, 1990). The human cost of this deductive failure was high: the deaths of many people, and the release of radiation 10 times that of the bomb dropped on Hiroshima. Deduction is a crucial form of everyday thought, and we can all be placed at risk by the sorts of errors that I have described, especially the failure to envisage alternative possibilities compatible with the facts. What is true, however, is that human reasoners are not usually interested in validity for its own sake. Their goal is to reach conclusions that are true and useful. They often lack sufficient information to reach a valid conclusion, and so are forced to go beyond the given information and to make an *induction*. The mental machinery underlying induction, as I show in the next chapter, is closely related to the mechanism for deduction.

2 Induction

Why do you keep your money in a bank? The answer is that you know from previous experience that the money will be safe, that the bank will honor your checks, and that it will not go bankrupt. These inferences are not deductively valid — as so often in life, you lack the information to reach such conclusions — but they are plausible *inductions*. Induction is, indeed, part of both everyday and scientific thinking. It enables us to understand the world and provides an ever-ready guide to people and their behavior, but induction is a risky business. One of the most momentous cognitive errors of the 20th-century was an inductive inference that was wrong. The engineers in charge at the Chernobyl power plant inferred that the explosion had not destroyed the reactor (Medvedev, 1990). They knew from previous experience that such an event was highly unlikely, and, at first, they had no evidence to the contrary. Their inference was initially plausible. As more evidence became available, however, they should have abandoned it. Two probationary engineers whom they had sent to examine the reactor returned with a report that the reactor was destroyed. Their observations cost them their lives. Firemen reported that large amounts of graphite were lying around the reactor building, and its only source was the reactor. Yet, the engineers did not abandon their inductive conclusion in the face of these signs to the contrary. They clung stubbornly to their belief that the reactor was intact, and this psychological fixation was a major cause of the appalling delay in evacuating the inhabitants of the nearby town and countryside. If human beings are to perform more skillfully, and if machines are to be clever enough to guide them, then we need a better theory of both the strengths and weaknesses of human inductive competence.

There is an enormous amount of confusion about induction. Some theorists restrict the term to very narrow cases; others use it to refer to any inferences that are not deductions. The authors of textbooks sometimes define it as leading from particular premises to general conclusions, in contrast to deduction, which they define as leading from general premises to particular conclusions. In fact, induction can lead from particular premises to a particular conclusion, and deduction from general premises to a general conclusion. I shall define induction in broad terms, and then distinguish different varieties of it: *an induction* is any process of thought yielding a conclusion that increases the semantic information in its initial observations or premises. In contrast, valid deduction never increases semantic information.

What, you may wonder, is semantic information? The idea goes back to medieval philosophers who argued that the more states of affairs that a proposition rules out as false the more information it conveys. In certain domains, semantic information can even be quantified (see Bar-Hillel & Carnap, 1964; Johnson-Laird, 1983). For example, consider the assertion, "There is a radiation leak or the dosimeter is faulty, or both." It has the following three models of alternative possibilities (see chapter 1):

$$
\begin{array}{cc}
r & f \\
r & \neg f \\
\neg r & f
\end{array}
$$

where r represents "there is a radiation leak", f represents "the dosimeter is faulty", and "$\neg$" represents negation. Each line denotes a model of a different situation, and so the disjunctive assertion eliminates only one out of the four possibilities: the situation where there is neither a radiation leak nor a faulty dosimeter, $\neg r \quad \neg f$. The categorical assertion, "There is a radiation leak," eliminates two models out of the four, $\neg r$ f, and $\neg r \quad \neg f$, and so it has a greater information content. The conjunction, "There is a radiation leak and the dosimeter is faulty," eliminates all but one of the four and so has a still higher information content. This notion of semantic information enables us to draw a simple distinction between deduction and induction.

Here is a case of deduction. You know:

There is a radiation leak or the dosimeter is faulty, or both.

By testing the dosimeter, you observe:

The dosimeter is not faulty.

And so you infer:

∴ There is a radiation leak.

The conclusion follows validly from your premises. It does not increase semantic information: the premises eliminate all but one possibility:

r   ¬ f

and the conclusion holds in this model too. Like any useful deduction, the conclusion makes explicit what was hitherto only implicit in the premises.
Here is a case of induction. You know, as before:

There is a radiation leak or the dosimeter is faulty, or both.

You observe:

The dosimeter is faulty.

And you infer:

∴ There is no radiation leak.

The conclusion does not follow validly from the premises. They eliminate all but two models:

  r   f
¬ r   f

The conclusion increases information beyond what is in the premises because it eliminates the first of these two models, yet the conclusion may be true. The difference between the two sorts of inference is, accordingly, that induction increases semantic information but deduction does not.
Semantic information must not be confused with truth. An assertion has semantic information because it eliminates certain possibilities *if* it is true. It may not be true, however, and neither deduction nor induction comes with any guarantee that their conclusions are true. If the conclusion you deduced about the radiation turns out to be false, then you will have to revise your belief in one or the other of the premises. If the conclusion you induced about the radiation turns out to be false, then you do not necessarily need to change your mind about the truth of the premises. A valid deduction yielding a false conclusion must be based on false premises, but an induction yielding a false conclusion need not be.

Deduction and induction do not exhaust the possible semantic relations between a set of premises and a conclusion. There are two other cases. First, the premises and the conclusion could fail to rule out any possibilities in common; that is, they could contradict one another. Although individuals may be guilty of entertaining self-contradictory sets of beliefs, no elementary inferential step leads directly from an assertion to its negation. Second, the premises and conclusion can rule out overlapping possibilities, that is, they rule out some states in common, but each, in addition, rules out further states. For instance, an individual thinks:

There is a radiation leak.

and then concludes:

There was an earthquake.

Both assertions rule out the situation:

$$\neg r \qquad \neg e$$

where "e" denotes the occurrence of an earthquake, but each assertion independently rules out other distinct situations. One special case of this sort, to which I return in chapter 3, is the *creation* of innovative concepts or conjectures.

By defining induction as a sort of thinking, I intend to exclude certain other processes. The evolution of a new species is similar to induction: it depends on the reproductive shuffling of genes and the action of natural selection. The classical conditioning of an animal is similar to induction: the animal learns the covariation between two classes of events, such as the sound of the dinner gong and the arrival of food. The learning of a skill such as skiing is similar to induction: the skier learns to coordinate various actions as a result of practice. Induction, however, concerns propositional knowledge: it is a question of *knowing that* rather than *knowing how*. It starts with propositions—a set of observations and a background of general knowledge—and its goal is a conclusion that increases knowledge in a plausible way, a conclusion that goes beyond the starting point in a way that is likely to be true. Induction depends, in part, on unconscious processes but it yields conscious knowledge.

Historically, there have been only two important ideas about induction. The first idea is that induction is a search for what is common to the members of a set. Hence, if all the positive instances of a concept have an element in common, then that element may define the concept. If the positive and negative instances of the concept differ just in respect of that element, then it *is* the critical element. These principles can be traced back to the British Empiricist philosophers (e.g., Mill, 1843/1950), and it is they who provided the blueprint for a generation of modern psychological investigations. For example, one of the founders of Behaviorism, Hull (1920), studied the acquisition of concepts based on common elements and extended the idea to everyday concepts, arguing that the meaning of *dog* is "a characteristic more or less common to all dogs and not common to cats, dolls, and teddy-bears". Children supposedly converge on the concept as a result of experiencing the word and the object in different pairings that allow them to infer the common element, a process that Hull took to be largely unconscious. Both the Russian psychologist Vygotsky and the Swiss psychologist Piaget held similar views. Their results led them to claim that young children lack the capacity for abstract thought that is needed to isolate the common elements of concepts (see Inhelder & Piaget, 1964; Vygotsky, 1934/1962).

The second idea rejects common elements (Smoke, 1932; Wittgenstein, 1953), and hence, dogs have nothing in common with one another. The criteria for doghood certainly include having four legs, fur, and the ability to bark, but these are not necessary conditions: a dog could be three-legged, bald, and mute. The criteria simply characterize a *prototypical* dog. This idea of prototypes led a secret life in psychology (see, e.g., Fisher, 1916) until it emerged in the work of Rosch (e.g., 1973). She argued that real entities, unlike those that had been studied in the psychological laboratory, have features that are correlated—feathers tend to be found on wings, scales on fins, and fur on limbs—and they are mentally represented by prototypes. This hypothesis was corroborated by the finding that not all instances of a concept are deemed to be equally representative—a terrier is a prototypical dog, but a chihuahua is not—and the time it takes to make judgments about instances of a concept depends on the distance of the instance from the prototype (Rips, Shoben, & Smith, 1973).

Rosch (1977) claimed that in any conceptual hierarchy, such as *terrier-dog-animal,* one level is basic. It is at this level that prototypes exist, that objects are initially categorized, and that instances of a concept have the most in common with one another and the least in common with other concepts at the same level. For example, *dog* is a basic-level concept: dogs typically have many properties that distinguish them from cats, such as their shape and behavior. One level up from *dog* is the concept of *animals,* and different animals have much less in common than different dogs. One level down from *dog* are *terriers,* but they have only a few additional features over and above those of dogs in general. Recent research has slightly altered this picture of concepts. In fact, individuals have prototypes at more than one level: they have a prototype for *dog* and a prototype for *terrier.* Likewise, the level at which objects are initially categorized varies from one concept to another, and from one person to another depending on their particular expertise in the domain: a dog breeder is likely to categorize dogs immediately in terms of their breeds (Joliecoeur, Gluck, & Kosslyn, 1984).

The contrast between common elements and prototypes is striking. The first idea presupposes that concepts have common elements, and the second idea rejects this presupposition. Not surprisingly, current studies of induction are in a state of flux. Students of artificial intelligence have turned the first idea into machines that manipulate explicitly structured symbols in order to acquire concepts; connectionists have implemented a version of the second idea; psychologists have examined both ideas experimentally; and philosophers have argued that neither idea is viable and that induction is impossible. Certainly, no complete theory of induction exists, and this gap is a serious defect in our knowledge.

The present chapter examines induction as it occurs in humans and machines. It aims to answer three questions: What are the varieties of induction? What are its underlying mechanisms? What are the conceptual elements on which it is based? The first half of the chapter is about induction. It begins with an analysis of the different varieties, and it distinguishes between inductions about specific events and inductions about general classes of events. It develops the theory that human induction depends on mental models rather than on a mental language analogous to predicate calculus. It deals first with specific inductions, and then, after an examination of machine induction, with general inductions. Despite the great variety of operations of generalization used by inductive machines to manipulate linguistic hypotheses, the chapter shows that induction requires just one operation on models. This operation has an unexpected effect, hitherto overlooked by the language-based theories, and it suffices for all inductive generalizations. The second half of the chapter is about concepts. It argues that the induction of novel concepts *is* possible — contrary to the strong doctrine of innate ideas — and it establishes the minimum of innate components necessary for such inductions. It proposes a new theory of concepts, and the mental components that underlie them, which fits prototypes and necessary-and-sufficient conditions into a common framework. Finally, it combines this theory with the operation on models in a proposal about the design of the human inductive mechanism.

The Varieties of Induction

Induction occurs in three stages that parallel the analysis of deduction in chapter 1. The first stage is to grasp some propositions, some verbal assertions or perceptual observations. The second stage is to frame a hypothesis that reaches a better description or understanding of this information in relation to a background of general knowledge. This conclusion may follow validly from the premises *and* the background knowledge, in which case the inference is not an induction but an *enthymeme,* that is, a deduction that depends on premises that are not stated explicitly (see Osherson, Smith, & Shafir, 1986). The conclusion of a genuine induction, however, goes beyond the initial semantic information. The third stage, if a reasoner is prudent, is to evaluate the conclusion and as a result, to maintain, modify, or abandon it. That is the general plan, but it encompasses many different sorts of induction, so I will begin with a survey of them.

A common form of induction in daily life concerns specific events:

I eat lobster, and later I feel ill.
I infer: I feel ill because the lobster upset my stomach.
Your colleague normally comes to work by train. Today, she came by
    car.
You infer: There is something wrong with the train service.
A man is arrested at a supermarket. The police find several cans of food
    in his inner pockets.
They infer: The cans were stolen.

These inductions go beyond the information given, but they concern only specific events—typically, the causes or reasons for them.

In contrast, another form of induction in daily life leads to a *general* conclusion. For instance, you vacation in London and learn the hard way the penalties for illegal parking:

If you park where there is at least one yellow line at the side of the road,
    they wheel-clamp your car or tow it away.

After a few journeys by air in the United States, you are likely to infer:

Internal flights are usually late.

After standing in line to no avail for just one occasion in Italy, you are likely to infer:

In Italian bars with cashiers, you pay the cashier first and then take your
    receipt to the bar to make your order.

A special case of an induction is an *explanation,* although not all explanations are arrived at inductively. In the preceding cases, induction yields mere descriptions that make no strong theoretical claims, but the process may be accompanied by a search for an explanation, for example:

Internal flights are usually late because too many planes are flying in and out of too few airports, and so, because they cannot all land and take off at the same time, they tend to get stacked up in the air and to form long lines on the ground.

The distinction between a description and an explanation is particularly important in scientific thinking. Scientific laws are general descriptions of phenomena: for instance, Kepler's third law of planetary motion describes the elliptical orbits of the planets. Scientific theories purport to explain these regularities on the basis of more fundamental considerations. Thus, Einstein's theory of gravitation explains planetary orbits in terms of the effects of mass on the curvature of space-time.

Some authors restrict the term *induction* to processes that yield descriptions and use *abduction* to refer to processes that yield explanations. Others argue that induction in this latter sense plays no significant role in scientific thinking. Thus, Popper (1972) claimed that science is based on explanatory hypotheses that are open to falsification, but he offered no account of their origins. The distinction between an explanation and a corresponding description is far from clear. One view is that the explanation is a statement in a theoretical language that logically implies the description, which is a statement in an observation language. This claim has been disputed (e.g., Harman, 1973), and it misses the heart of the matter psychologically.

You can describe a phenomenon without understanding it, but you cannot explain a phenomenon unless you have some putative understanding of it. A descriptive mental model of the phenomenon merely simulates it, although such a model may be useful in predicting certain events. An explanatory model of the phenomenon, however, embodies underlying principles, so even if it is incomplete or partially erroneous, it is more powerful than a simulation. If you have an explanatory model, you may know what causes the phenomenon; what results from it; how to influence, control, initiate, or prevent it; how it relates to other phenomena or how it resembles them; how to predict its onset and course; what its internal or underlying structure is; how to diagnose unusual events; and, in science, how to relate the domain as a whole to others. Scientific explanations characteristically make use of theoretical notions that are unobservable or that are at a lower physical level than descriptions of the phenomena. An explanation accounts for what you do not understand in terms of what you do understand: you cannot construct a model if the key explanatory concepts are not available to you. Hence, a critical distinction is whether an explanation is developed by deduction (without increasing the semantic information in the premises and background knowledge), by induction (increasing the semantic information), or by creation (with an overlap in the semantic information in the explanation and the original knowledge and premises).

The induction of a generalization could just as well be described as an induction about a concept. In the previous examples, you acquired knowledge about the concepts:

parking violations in London
internal flights in the United States
Italian bars with cashiers

These ad hoc concepts are clearly put together out of ordinary concepts, such as those for planes, cars, and bars. Adults continue to learn concepts throughout their lives. Some are acquired from knowledge by acquaintance, others from knowledge by description. You cannot acquire the full concept of a color, a wine, or a sculpture without a direct acquaintance with them, but you can learn about quarks, genes, and the unconscious from descriptions of them.

In summary, inductions are either specific or general, and either descriptive or explanatory. Generalizations include the acquisition of ad hoc concepts by encountering instances of them, and the formulation of hypotheses to explain sets of observations, even perhaps a set containing just a single datum: Sir Alexander Fleming observed the destruction of bacteria on a culture plate, an observation that led him to infer that a causal agent had destroyed the bacteria, and thence to the discovery of penicillin. All of these results are fallible, but human reasoners can be aware of the fallibility of their inductions. So much for the variety of inductions. We turn now to a model analysis of them.

MODELS AND SPECIFIC INDUCTIONS

The central idea in the theory of mental models is that the process of understanding yields a model. In deduction, if a model supports a conclusion, then it can be tested by searching for alternative models. Often, however, the process of constructing a model increases semantic information. In the case of specific inductions in everyday life, the process of inference is hardly separable as a distinct mental activity: it is part of the normal business of making sense of the world. A critical factor in the construction of the model is the *availability* of relevant knowledge, which, as Tversky and Kahneman (1973) have shown, can bias judgment. For example, most people judge that words beginning with the letter "r" are more frequent than words in which "r" occurs as the third letter. They are wrong, but it is easier to think of words beginning with "r" than words in which it occurs third. How knowledge is represented and triggered during comprehension is deeply puzzling. There is no shortage of conjectures (e.g., Schank, 1986), but no one has explained, in principle, how one thought rather than its individual concepts can trigger another. Even when the process is geared to an explanatory goal, it does not necessarily abide by logical principles. When the starter won't turn over the engine, your immediate thought is:

The battery is dead.

Your conclusion is plausible but invalid, and so Polya (1957) has suggested that formal, but invalid, rules are the basis of such inductions. Because formal rules do not appear to underlie valid inferences (see chapter 1), it seems more likely that specific inductions have another basis.

One possibility is that knowledge is represented by a "production system" made up of a vast set of conditional rules (see Anderson, 1983; Newell, 1990). The triggering of these rules, however, is slightly problematic for induction. A piece of general knowledge can be represented by a conditional rule:

If a car's battery is dead, then the starter won't turn over the engine.

A rule is triggered by the satisfaction of its antecedent condition, and so this rule will be triggered by the observation:

The car's battery is dead.

To use this rule invalidly, it is necessary for it also to be triggered by its consequent, and, as a result to assert its antecedent. But, in such a system, the rule expresses a biconditional that is too strong:

If, and only if, a car's engine won't turn over, then its battery is flat.

A more radical possibility is that knowledge is represented directly in the form of models. You have a model, perhaps simplistic, of the car's electrical circuitry, including the battery and starter:

The three symbols in the brackets on the left denote the battery with power, the circuit conveying power to the starter, and the starter as working. The symbol on right denotes the starter turning over the engine. The three dots represent an implicit model of an alternative possibility. You perceive that the starter does not turn over the engine, and this observation eliminates the first model and fleshes out the implicit model to yield:

You can, accordingly, diagnose that the battery has no power (or that the circuit is broken, or that the starter does not work). The original model might be triggered by anything in working memory that matches its explicit content, and so it can be used to make both deductions and inductions.

When you construct other models, you put them together out of existing models: you imagine, say, a pink elephant and a soft tomato, and then you combine the two in some relation: the elephant is eating the tomato or it sits down on the tomato. The process is analogous to understanding a verbal description of the events. The constituents are concepts: concepts of entities in the world, such as an elephant and a tomato, concepts of relations between them, such as eating and sitting, concepts of properties of objects, such as pink and soft, but when you imagine such scenarios, your knowledge also fleshes out the models with many additional details. The process is automatic, involuntary, and unconscious. When you imagine the elephant eating the tomato, you think of it picking the tomato up with its trunk. When you imagine the elephant sitting down on the tomato, you think of the tomato being flattened.

People can be extraordinarily imaginative in finding explanatory connections between events. Tony Anderson and I demonstrated this ability in an unpublished experiment based on randomly paired events. In one condition, the subjects received pairs of sentences taken at random from separate stories:

John made his way to a shop which sold TV sets.
Celia had recently had her ears pierced.

In another condition, the sentences were modified to make them co-referential:

Celia made her way to a shop which sold TV sets.
She had recently had her ears pierced.

The subjects' task was to explain what was going on. They readily went beyond the given information to account for what was happening. They proposed, for example, that Celia was getting reception in her earrings and wanted the TV shop to investigate, that she was wearing new earrings and wanted to see herself on closed circuit TV, that she had won a bet by having her ears pierced and was going to spend the money on a TV set, and so on. The subjects were almost as equally ingenious with the sentences that were not co-referential.

Anderson and I investigated another aspect of specific inductions in an experiment using such premises as:

The old man was bitten by a poisonous snake.
There was no known antidote.

When we asked the subjects to say what happened, every one replied that the old man died, but when the experimenter responded, "Yes, that's possible but not in fact true," then the majority of subjects were able to envisage alternative scenarios in which the old man did not die. If the experimenter gave the same response to each of the subjects' subsequent ideas, sooner or later they ran out of ideas. Yet, subjects generated ideas in roughly the same order; that is, the sequences were reliably correlated. The availability of relevant knowledge has some consistency within the culture. The conclusions to the snake-bite problem, for instance, tended to occur in the following order:

1. The old man died.
2. The poison was successfully removed (e.g., by sucking it out).
3. The old man was immune to the poison.
4. The poison was weak and not deadly.
5. The poison was blocked from entering the circulatory system (e.g., by the man's thick clothing).

Could the subjects be certain that they had exhausted all possible models of the premises? Of course not. Indeed, by the end of the experiment, the subjects' confidence in their initial conclusion had fallen reliably, even in a second group where the experimenter merely responded, "Yes, that's possible," to each idea. These sorts of inferences, which often crop up in everyday life, are not *deductively closed,* because of a lack of sufficient information to determine that their conclusions are valid. Specific inductions are potentially unlimited, and so there may always be some other, as yet unforeseen, counterexample to a putative conclusion. A few of the subjects in the experiment produced still more recondite possibilities, such as that the old man was kept alive long enough for someone to invent an antidote. The sequence of conclusions can be generated by manipulations of a model of the circulation of the blood, the effect of toxins on the heart, and so on (see Bara, Carassa, & Geminiani, 1984, for a computer implementation).

GENERAL INDUCTIONS

Machines for Induction

The origin of machines for induction is probably Bruner, Goodnow, and Austin's (1956) seminal account of strategies for identifying novel concepts. Their subjects had to induce ad hoc concepts such as "two green triangles." They were given an initial positive instance of the concept. They then chose instances, one by one, from an array in front of them, and were told whether or not each choice was an instance of the concept. They continued until they were able to identify the concept. One strategy described by Bruner et al. is to keep track of all hypotheses currently compatible with evidence, and to choose instances that eliminate as many hypotheses as possible (*simultaneous scanning*). A less burdensome strategy is to consider a single hypothesis at a time, to select positive instances of it, and to adopt a new hypothesis only if the current hypothesis is disconfirmed (*successive scanning*). Another possibility is to focus on the initial positive instance, say, two large green triangles with a single border, and then to choose instances that differ from it either on a single attribute (*conservative focussing*) or on several attributes (*focus gambling*). If the new instance is also a member of the concept, then the attributes on which it differs from the focus are irrelevant. If the new instance is not a member of the concept, then the changed attributes are critical. When a reasoner has been conservative and changed only one attribute (e.g., two large *red* triangles with a single border), the original property is part of the definition of the concept. But, when the reasoner has gambled by changing several attributes (e.g., *one small red square* with a single border), the gamble has failed, because of the difficulty in determining which of the changed properties is crucial. These strategies are appropriate for concepts defined in terms of a conjunction of common elements. They are less appropriate for concepts defined in terms of a disjunction of elements, but such concepts proved to be harder to learn — a fact that was taken to corroborate the psychological reality of the strategies.

The first explicit efforts to design a program for machine induction continued in the same tradition of Boolean concepts, that is, those that can be defined in terms of the negation, conjunction, and disjunction of properties. (The propositional calculus is an alternative interpretation of the same Boolean algebra.) Hunt and his colleagues devised a series of programs, CLS, that could learn any Boolean concept whatsoever (Hunt, Marin, & Stone, 1966). The basic program constructs a decision tree for categorizing instances. It works top–down by choosing an attribute, dividing the instances into subsets according to the different values of this attribute, and then applying the same algorithm recursively to each of these subsets until each has been divided into positive and negative instances of the concept. Hence, the program has three principal steps:

1. It eliminates any irrelevant attributes, that is, those with a value that is common to all the positive and negative instances of the concept.
2. It adds a node to the decision tree if a value of an attribute is common to all positive instances and to no negative instances of the concept.
3. Otherwise, it adds a node to the decision tree if a value of an attribute is common to all positive instances or, failing that, to at least some positive instances. It then make recursive calls applying exactly the same program to the subsets on each branch.

The recursions are the heart of the program, and they can be best illustrated by an example. Suppose the following four figures, which are defined in terms of two binary variables, shape and color, are the positive and negative instances of a concept:

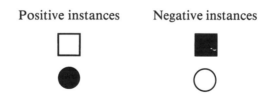

Positive instances   Negative instances

Step 1 fails because there are no irrelevant attributes; step 2 fails because nothing is common to all the positive instances. Hence, step 3 selects square as a property of at least one positive instance. The first node in the decision tree therefore concerns shape, and the stimuli are divided into those that are squares and those that are circles. The algorithm is then applied recursively, first to the square subset:

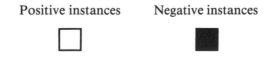

Positive instances   Negative instances

Step 2 selects color, because its values distinguish between the positive and negative instances of the square subset. Finally, the algorithm is applied recursively to the circle subset that emerged from the first decision, and again color distinguishes between the positive and negative instances. Figure 2 shows the final decision tree.

The decision-tree procedure has inspired various more powerful programs, notably ID3, which uses an information-theoretic measure in order to make an optimal choice of attributes to test (Quinlan, 1983). Decision-tree machines treat everything as the values of attributes. The attributes can be complex (e.g., the distance from the black king to the knight in a chess position), but there is no direct way to represent relations.

Boolean concepts are too simple. They depart from reality in several ways. Most importantly, the concepts of daily life usually depend on relations that cannot even be expressed within a Boolean framework. A dog is not a conjunction of head, body, legs, and tail: its legs *support* its body, its tail *is connected to* its body, and so on. Children acquire such relational concepts much more easily than they acquire Boolean concepts (Markman & Seibert, 1976). They can also be acquired by a program developed by Winston (1975) that concerns a simple imaginary world of toy blocks. The program requires a human teacher to provide a helpful sequence of positive instances and "near misses," negative instances that are nearly positive. It begins by forming a hypothesis based on the initial positive instance that the teacher provides. It represents the hypothesis in a semantic network that encodes relations and properties as follows (ignoring the syntax of networks):

A cube with the property of being large supports a cylinder with the property of being small.

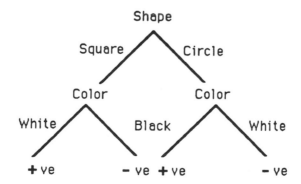

FIG. 2. A decision-tree constructed by Hunt's program for the concept defined in the text

If the teacher provides a near miss, then the program uses it to establish the necessity for some property or relation. For example, given a near miss in which the large cube is *next* to the small cylinder, then the program modifies its hypothesis to:

A cube . . . must support a cylinder . . .

If a positive instance does not match the current hypothesis, then the program attempts to generalize the hypothesis so as to accommodate it. Given a positive instance in which the cube supports a *rectangular column,* it must either use a superordinate term or else a disjunction:

A cube . . . must support a cylinder . . . or a column . . .

There may be several ways to generalize the concept, in which case only one is followed up and the rest are stored for future use. If the program arrives at a point where it is unable to find a consistent generalization, then it returns to the list of these stored alternatives to try a new possibility.

The use of near misses bears out a classic observation by Smoke (1933) that they make learning easier, but the program would have difficulty in coping with negative instances that were not near misses. It cannot deal with negative instances that differ in several ways from its current hypothesis. It is geared to finding conjunctive descriptions, and it uses various rules of generalization, including moving up to a superordinate term in the semantic network.

The representational language for machine induction was finally extended to a version of the predicate calculus by Michalski and his colleagues. Their program, INDUCE 1.2, finds a maximally specific conjunctive description of a concept, that is, a description containing the most conjuncts that are true of all of the concept's known instances (Dietterich & Michalski, 1983; Michalski, 1973). The program distinguishes relations (e.g., connected to) from properties (e.g., red), and first searches for plausible generalizations about relations, and then for those about properties. The search uses various rules of generalization to develop a set of candidate hypotheses. One such rule drops a conjunct from a defining condition. It transforms the description:

If it is a cube & it is green then it is an instance of the concept.

into:

if it is a cube then it is an instance of the concept.

The resulting hypotheses that cover all the positive instances of the concept are removed from the search process and put into the set of putative maximally specific descriptions; when this set reaches a predetermined size, the search halts. Once the relations have been taken into account, each putative maximally specific description is filled out by finding the concept's properties from another similar search. (I discuss other rules of generalization further on.)

The space of possible generalizations distinguishing between positive and negative instances grows very rapidly, and this so-called "version space" of hypotheses soon becomes too large to be maintained in its entirety. A sensible procedure pioneered by Mitchell (1977) is to maintain a record of only the most specific and the most general descriptions in the version space. If you are a subject in an induction experiment, and I tell you that:

tall dark handsome

is an instance of a concept concerning individuals, then, assuming a simple conjunctive concept based on binary values of attributes, the most specific description in the version space is "tall, dark, and handsome individuals", and the most general is "any individual." If I then tell you that:

tall dark ugly

is also an instance of the concept, you need to adjust the most specific description by moving up the version space to a slightly more general description, "tall and dark individuals." If I then tell you that:

short dark handsome

is *not* an instance of the concept, you need to adjust the most general description by moving down the version space to the slightly more specific description, "tall individuals." Of course, there may be more than one maximally specific or maximally general description in the version space, but as new positive instances are encountered, the most specific descriptions are forced toward the more general; and as new negative instances are encountered, the most general descriptions are forced toward the more specific. Induction is a process of converging on the right description — not too general, and not too specific.

The state of the art in machine induction can be summarized succinctly. Machines represent inductive hypotheses in an internal language based on a given set of concepts; they use a variety of linguistic operations for generalizing (and specializing) these hypotheses; there are, as yet, no machines that can rapidly and invariably converge on the correct inductive description in a language as powerful as the predicate calculus. No machine can induce the concept of motion possessed by a 2-month-old infant (Spelke, 1991), let alone the concept of motion possessed by a physicist.

Generalization and Specialization

In the search for a true descriptive induction about a domain, the relevant concepts must be available. Once they are in the pool of available ideas, there are two ways in which an inductive hypothesis can err. It can be too general or too specific. These notions seem straightforward but, in fact, they are quite tricky. To clarify them, we will consider some simple examples.

Suppose that you hypothesize that the concept in an experiment is:

black squares

If this hypothesis is too specific, then it excludes instances of the concept (e.g., if the real concept is squares in general). Conversely, if the hypothesis is too general, then it includes instances that are not in the concept (e.g., if the real concept is large black squares). A typical operation of generalization, which is often used in inductive programs (e.g., Winston, 1984, chap. 11), is to drop a clause from a conjunctive antecedent of a conditional. Given the initial hypothesis describing the instances of an unknown concept, such as:

If it is black and square, then it is an instance of the concept.

this operation of generalization leads to a new hypothesis:

If it is square, then it is an instance of the concept.

When this operation is carried out in reverse, it transforms a hypothesis into one that is more specific.

Intuitive judgments about generalization become difficult for more complicated transformations. Consider, for example, the operation that transforms this hypothesis about ice:

If something is ice, then it is water.

into:

If something is ice, then it is water and it is frozen.

Is this operation one of generalization or of specialization? On the one hand, it expresses more specific properties of ice; on the other hand, it seems, as Michalski (1983, pp. 104–105) argued, to yield a more general description.

The way to clarify inductive operations is to consider their effect on semantic information. An operation is a generalization if, and only if, it increases the semantic information in the hypothesis about the concept, so that the resulting proposition rules out as false at least one contingency that was not ruled out by the original proposition. The hypothesis:

If it is black and square, then it is an instance of the concept.

eliminates only one sort of possibility: a black square that is not an instance of the concept. The new hypothesis:

If it is square, then it is an instance of the concept.

eliminates the same possibility, and in addition a white square that is not an instance of the concept. Conversely, an operation is a specialization if, and only if, it decreases semantic information. Because any operation that decreases semantic information is valid, it follows that specialization is just a special case of valid deduction.

One must be careful to distinguish between a proposition that explicitly describes a concept:

If it is black and square, then it is an instance of the concept.

and the simple noun phrase that refers to the corresponding set:

black squares

A proposition is either true or false, whereas a noun phrase does not have a truth value, but rather is either satisfied or not by a particular set of objects. The effect of generalization on a proposition is to eliminate possible states of affairs, but the effect of generalization on a noun phrase is to admit more members to the set. The description "black squares" is satisfied by the following set:

The description "squares" is a generalization and it is satisfied by a set with additional members:

In summary, the generalization of a proposition rules out more possibilities as false, but the generalization of a set is satisfied by more possibilities. This difference is a potential source of confusion, leading to inconsistencies in the use of the terms, *generalization* and *specialization*.

Models and the Operation of Generalization in a Boolean Domain

How many different operations of generalization (and specialization) are there? Figure 3 shows some of the rules of generalization that have been used in programs for induction, but they by no means exhaust the set of possible rules. A simple hypothesis about a concept is:

If it is a square then it is an instance of the concept.

where the antecedent is a sufficient condition for the concept. An alternative hypothesis has the form:

If it is an instance of the concept then it is a square.

where the consequent is a necessary condition for the concept. Sufficient conditions for a concept, C, can be generalized by the following operations:

1. Dropping a conjunct from the antecedent:
   If A & B then C   becomes   *If A then C*
2. Adding a disjunct to the antecedent:
   If A then C   becomes   *If A or B then C*

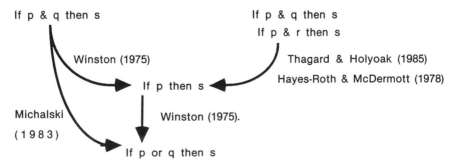

FIG. 3.   Some rules of generalization used in inductive programs.

where "or" symbolizes an inclusive disjunction. Necessary conditions for a concept, C, can be generalized by the following operations:

  3. Adding a conjunct to the consequent:
     If C then A   becomes   *If C then (A & B)*
  4. Dropping a disjunct from the consequent:
     If C then (A or B)   becomes   *If C then A*

Both conditionals can be generalized by adding the respective converse so as to state necessary and sufficient conditions:

  5. Adding the converse conditional:
     If A then C ⎫
     If C then A ⎭   become   *If and only if A then C*

These transformations are applicable to inductive hypotheses in general. Hence, the step from:

  If something is ice, then it is water.

to:

  If something is ice, then it is water and it is frozen.

is indeed a generalization, which depends on operation 3.

  The five operations just listed do not constitute an exhaustive set of all possible generalizations. Consider, for example, the set of the four possible ways in which the proposition, "it's a square," or its negation, could be related to the proposition, "it's a positive instance of the concept," or its negation:

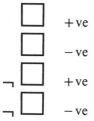

$\quad$ +ve

$\quad$ −ve

$\quad$ +ve

$\quad$ −ve

where "¬" symbolizes negation, "+ve" symbolizes "it's a positive instance of the concept," and "−ve" symbolizes "it's a negative instance of the concept." The number of relevant propositions, n, is two in this case, the number of possible models is 2^n, and the number of possible subsets of them is $2^{(2^n)}$, including both the set as a whole and the empty set. With any set of models based on n propositions, then the hypothesis:

If it's a square then it's a positive instance of the concept.

eliminates one quarter of them. We can now ask how many logically distinct propositions are generalizations of this hypothesis, that is, how many eliminate the same models plus at least one additional model. The answer equals the number of different sets of models that exclude the same quarter of possible models as the original hypothesis minus two other cases: the empty set of models (which corresponds to a self-contradiction) and the set excluded by the original hypothesis itself:

$$2^{(2^n - (0.25)(2^n))} - 2$$

In general, given a hypothesis, H, that rules out a proportion, I(H), of possible models, the number of possible generalizations of H is equal to:

$$2^{(2^n - (I(H))(2^n))} - 2$$

What this formula shows is that unless a hypothesis has a very high information content, which rules out a large proportion of models, the number of its possible generalizations increases exponentially with the number, n, of potentially relevant propositions. Any simple search procedure based on eliminating putative hypotheses will not be computationally tractable. It will be unable to examine all possible generalizations in a reasonable time. Many inductive machines have been designed without taking this problem into account. They are viable only because the domain of generalization has been kept artificially small. The programmer, rather than the machine, has determined the members of the set of relevant propositions.

Although there are many possible generalizations of an inductive hypothesis, the number of *operations* required to make these generalizations is very much smaller. In fact, only one operation is needed for all the generalizations in Fig. 3 and, indeed, for all possible generalizations in a Boolean domain. It is the operation of adding information that is inconsistent with an existing model. This information thereby eliminates the model. To revert to the five operations that I discussed earlier, the generalization of dropping a conjunct from an antecedent consists in eliminating one model. Thus, an assertion of the form:

If A & B then C

is equivalent to a set of models that includes:

A $\neg$ B $\neg$ C

When this model is eliminated, the resulting set is equivalent to:

If A then C, and B or not-B

but an assertion of the form, B or not-B, is a tautology, so it can be dropped from the description to yield:

If A then C

The operation of adding information to a set of models can be used repeatedly. It suffices for any inductive generalization, because generalization is nothing more than the elimination of possible states of affairs. The resulting set of models can then be described by a parsimonious proposition. Although the operation obviates the need to choose among an indefinite number of different forms of linguistic generalization, it does not affect the intractability of the search. The problem now is to determine which models to eliminate, and, as ever, the number of possibilities to be considered increases exponentially with the number of models representing the initial situation.

Models and the Operation of Generalization in a Quantified Domain

Some inductive programs, such as INDUCE 1.2 (Michalski, 1983), operate in a domain that allows quantification over individuals, with a version of the predicate calculus. Where quantifiers range over infinitely many individuals, it is impossible to calculate semantic information on the basis of cardinalities, but it is still possible to maintain a partial rank order of generalization: one assertion is a generalization of another if it eliminates certain states of affairs over and above those eliminated by the initial assertion. Once again, we can ask, how many distinct operations of generalization are there?

The answer is that the only operation that we need is the archetypal one that adds information to models so as to eliminate otherwise possible states of affairs. From the standpoint of *linguistic* generalizations, however, the effects of adding information to a model can have strikingly different consequences. For example, you observe that some entities of a particular sort have a property in common:

Electrons emitted in radioactive decay damage the body.

Positrons emitted in radioactive decay damage the body.
Photons emitted in radioactive decay damage the body.

These initial observations support the following model:

    p   d
    p   d
    p   d
      . . .

where "p" symbolizes a radioactive particle and "d" damage to the body. Information can be added to the model to indicate that radioactive particles are exhaustively represented (see chapter 1):

    [p]   d
    [p]   d
    [p]   d
       . . .

This model rules out the possibility of any particles emitted in radioactive decay that do not damage the body. The corresponding linguistic operation leads from the initial observations to the conclusion:

Any particle emitted in radioactive decay damages the body.

Some authors refer to this inductive operation as *instance-based generalization* (Thagard & Holyoak, 1985) or as *turning constants into variables* (Michalski, 1983, p. 107). Given the operation of adding information to models, however, there is no need for rules that generalize linguistic expressions.

Information can be added to a model to represent a new property of existing individuals. If you have established the existence of individuals that satisfy one condition, then you make a generalization that they satisfy another condition. You observe, for example, some bees with an unusually potent sting:

    [s]
    [s]
    [s]
     . . .

where "s" denotes a bee with a potent sting, and the set is exhaustively represented. Further observations lead you to conjecture:

[m]   [s]
[m]   [s]
[m]   [s]
  . . .

where "m" denotes a certain mutation in the bees' genetic structure. This step is sometimes known as an abduction because it is an inductive hypothesis that is intended to explain an observed property: the cause of the potent sting is the mutation (see Peirce, 1958).

A new relation can be added between existing entities in a model. For example, a model might represent the relations among, say, a set of viruses and a set of symptoms. The semantically weakest case is as follows:

v   s

v   s

v ⟶ s

where there is one definite causal relation, signified by the arrow, but nothing is known about the relations, positive or negative, between the remaining pairwise combinations of viruses and symptoms. You can describe this model in the following terms:

At least one virus causes at least one of the symptoms.

By the addition of further causal relations the model may be transformed into the following one:

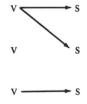

You can describe a model of this sort in the following terms:

Each of the symptoms is caused by at least one of the viruses.

Hence, the effect now is equivalent to the linguistic operation of replacing an existential quantifier (*at least one*) in the previous description by a universal quantifier (*each*). The addition of a further causal link yields a still stronger model:

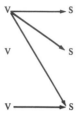

You can describe a model of this sort in the following terms:

At least one of the viruses causes each of the symptoms.

In the predicate calculus, the effect of the operator is to promote an existential quantifier ($\exists v$) from inside to outside the scope of a universal quantifier ($\forall s$):

$$\forall s \; \exists v \; v \text{ causes } s \Rightarrow \exists v \; \forall s \; v \text{ causes } s$$

No such rule, however, appears to be used by any current inductive machines. The model theory has therefore led us to a hitherto unused form of linguistic generalization.

The operation of adding information to models enables us to generalize from the weakest possible model to the strongest possible one in which each of the viruses causes each of the symptoms. The elimination of a model, as I noted earlier, is equivalent to adding information that contradicts the model. Hence, the addition of information to models suffices for all possible generalizations in those everyday domains that can be described by the predicate calculus.

How Can Induction be Constrained?

The burden of the argument so far is simple: induction is a search for a model that is consistent with observation and background knowledge. It calls for only one operation, but the search will be intractable where it is impossible to examine all possible effects of the operation. The way to cut the problem down to a reasonable size is not to search blindly by trial and error, but to use constraints to guide the search (Newell & Simon, 1972).

Three constraints can be used in any domain and may be built into the inductive mechanism itself: specificity, availability, and parsimony.

Specificity is a powerful constraint on induction. It is always helpful to frame the most specific hypothesis consistent with observation and background knowledge, that is, the hypothesis that admits the fewest possible instances of a concept. This constraint is essential when you can observe only positive instances of the concept. For example, if you encounter a patient infected with a new virus, and this individual has a fever, a sore throat, and a rash, then the most specific hypothesis about the signs of the disease is:

fever & sore throat & rash

If you now encounter another patient with the same viral infection, who has a fever and a rash, but no sore throat, you will realize that your initial hypothesis was too specific. You can generalize it to one consistent with the evidence:

fever & rash

Suppose, however, that you had started off with the more general inclusive disjunction:

fever or sore throat or rash

Although this hypothesis is consistent with the data, it is too general, so it would remain unaffected by your encounter with the second patient. If the only genuine sign of the disease is the rash, then you would never find out from positive examples alone, because your hypothesis would accommodate all of them. Hence, when you are trying to induce a concept from positive instances, you must follow the specificity constraint. Your hypothesis may admit too few instances, but if so, sooner or later, you will encounter a positive instance that will allow you to correct it.

This principle has been proposed by Berwick (1986) in terms of what he calls the "subset" principle, which he derived from a theorem in formal learning theory due to Anguin (1978). In elucidating children's acquisition of syntax, phonology, and concepts — domains in which they are likely to encounter primarily positive instances — Berwick argued that the instances that are described by a current inductive hypothesis should be as few as possible. If they are a proper subset of the actual set of instances, then children can correct their inductive hypothesis from encounters with further positive instances, but if the current hypothesis embraces all the members of the actual set and more, then it will be impossible for positive instances to refute the hypothesis. What Angluin proved was that positive instances could be used to identify a language in the limit, to converge upon its grammar without the need for subsequent modifications (see Gold, 1967), provided that the candidate hypotheses about the grammar could be ordered in the same way. In other words, it must be possible to construct a version space in which each successively more general hypothesis includes items that are not included in its predecessor. The inductive system can then start with the most specific hypothesis and move to a more general one whenever it encounters a positive instance that falls outside its current hypothesis.

Availability is another general constraint on induction. It arises from the machinery that underlies the retrieval of pertinent knowledge. Some information comes to mind more readily than other information, and the availability of information, as I mentioned earlier, can bias judgement. It also underlies the *mutability* of an event, the ease with which one can envisage a counterfactual scenario in which the event does *not* occur (see Kahneman & Miller, 1986; Tversky & Kahneman, 1982). Availability is a form of bias, but bias is what is needed to deal with the intractable nature of induction.

Parsimony is a matter of fewer concepts in fewer combinations. It can be defined only with respect to a given set of concepts and a system in which to combine them. Hence, it is easily defined for the propositional calculus, and there are programs guaranteed in principle to deliver maximally parsimonious descriptions of models within this domain (see Johnson-Laird, 1990). What complicates parsimony is that the presumption of a conceptual system begs the question. There is unlikely to be any procedure for determining absolute parsimony. Its role in induction therefore seems to be limited to comparisons among alternative theories framed within the same conceptual system.

I have left the most important constraint on induction until last for reasons that will become clear. It is the use of existing knowledge. A rich theory of the relevant domain cuts down the number of possible inductions; it may even allow an individual to generalize on the strength of only a single instance. This idea underlies so-called "explanation-based learning," in which a program uses its background knowledge of the domain to deduce why a particular instance is a member of a concept (DeJong & Mooney, 1986; Mitchell, Keller, & Kedar-Cabelli, 1986). Another source of knowledge is a helpful teacher. A teacher who cannot describe a concept may still be able to arrange for a suitable sequence of instances to be presented to pupils. This pedagogical technique cuts down the search space and enables limited inductive mechanisms to acquire concepts.

The constraints of theory are so important that they often override the pure inductive process: one simply ignores counterexamples to the theory.

The 18th-century German scientist and aphorist, Georg Lichtenberg, remarked: "One should not take notice of contradictory experiences until there are enough of them to make constructing a new system worthwhile." The molecular biologist James Watson has similarly observed that no *good* model ever accounts for all the facts because some data are bound to be misleading if not plain wrong (see Crick, 1988, p. 60). This methodological prescription appears to be observed automatically by young children seeking to acquire new concepts. Karmiloff-Smith and Inhelder (1974/1975) observed that children ignore counterexamples to their current hypotheses about how to balance beams. Such neglect of evidence implies that induction plays only a limited role in the development of explanations. The resulting explanation does not increase the semantic information in the observations, but rather eliminates possibilities that only overlap with those that the evidence eliminates. The process is therefore not inductive, but creative. I shall return to the creation of explanations in chapter 3, but to make sense of it, I need first to take up the topic of the second half of this chapter: the nature of concepts.

CAN CONCEPTS BE LEARNED?

Concepts are the building blocks of thought. Without them, induction would be impossible because everything would be unique. Different things have to be treated as the same for some purposes, and similar things have to be treated as different for other purposes. Concepts provide the system for classifying, subdividing, and interrelating things. The inductive machines described in the first half of this chapter construct new concepts out of old by using evidence to increase semantic information. These machines have all been built on the assumption that knowledge by acquaintance — encounters with specific instances of a concept — are the only way to proceed. Likewise, they take for granted an existing basis of concepts without worrying about its nature. The goal of the following sections is to formulate a theory of human concepts, that is, a theory of what concepts represent, how they represent it, and what their constituents are. The path will then be clear to describe the design of the human inductive mechanism. I must begin, however, with a question of overriding importance: Can concepts be learned?

The Composition of New Concepts

To answer the question of whether concepts can be learned, we need to understand how they relate to thoughts, or at least to those thoughts that have a propositional content. This relation is made manifest in the way in which words relate to sentences. A declarative sentence taken in context can express a thought that has a propositional content, that is, it can express a proposition that is either true or false. The individual concepts from which the thought is composed have, not truth values, but conditions of satisfaction. For example, the relational concept:

x is on the right of y

is satisfied by certain values of x and y. It is satisfied, for example, by the circle and triangle in the following arrangement:

△   ○

It is not satisfied by other arrangements, such as when you turn the page upside down. The noun phrases of a sentence convey concepts, and when the entities that satisfy these concepts also satisfy the relation, such as:

The circle is on the right of the triangle.

then the corresponding proposition is true. Hence, the thought that is expressed by uttering a sentence depends on the concepts corresponding to the words in the sentence and on how these words are combined grammatically.

The thought can be built up *compositionally,* that is it is composed from concepts by combining them in certain ways. The building blocks are the concepts corresponding to the meanings of words. The methods of composing them are the conceptual combinations corresponding to grammatical relations. Each rule in the grammar has a corresponding semantic principle for conceptual combination (see Dowty, Wall, & Peters, 1981). These methods of combination ensure, for example, that the correct concepts are assigned as the arguments of the relation, much as one computational procedure calls another as a subprocedure. There is one caveat: the thought conveyed by a sentence almost always depends in part on the context in which it is uttered, and contextual effects may violate compositionality.

Just as concepts combine to make thoughts, so thoughts can in turn make new concepts. For example, given the concepts of *building, column, part of,* and a few interstitial notions such as quantification, you can entertain the thought:

Columns are a part of some buildings.

This thought enables you to construct a noun phrase corresponding to the concept of a certain sort of entity:

buildings that have columns as a part

Given the further concepts of *equality* and *distance,* you can entertain the thought:

Some columned buildings have equal distances between their columns.

This thought then enables you to construct the concept:

buildings with equidistant columns

which, together with some further concepts, enables you to entertain the thought:

In some buildings with equidistant columns, the distance between the columns is at least four times the diameter of the columns.

The process can continue indefinitely, but this last thought yields the concept of a complex property:

having equidistant columns with a distance between them of at least four times the diameter of the columns

A single English adjective expresses this concept: *araeostyle*. There is, in short, a mutual dependence between concepts and thoughts: concepts are used to construct thoughts, which in turn are used to construct concepts, and on and on.

The most sustained examination of the composition of meanings is to be found in the work of Montague (1974) and his followers. Montague's theory was intended to be general enough to apply to any logically possible language, but to be as parsimonious as possible. Hence, starting from two primitive concepts, entity and truth, he showed how arbitrarily complex concepts can be built up as functions from one sort of concept to another; for example, a property is a function from entities to truth values because, for a given entity, the property is either true or false. The human conceptual system, as we shall see, is more bountiful in its ontological assumptions.

The Theory of Recursive Functions

The construction of new concepts out of old occurs transparently in the case of recursive functions. In order to see how concepts could be learned, we shall make an excursion into this branch of logic. It makes explicit the minimal theoretical machinery required to carry out any computation (see Boolos & Jeffrey, 1989). The theory constructs computational procedures out of three sorts of building blocks, which are called *functions* because they produce a unique output for any input:

1. The zero function, which produces the same constant value, 0, for an input of any natural number.
2. The successor function, which adds 1 to any natural number (e.g., the successor of 0 is 1).
3. The identity functions, which can return the identity of any member in a list; that is, one such function returns the first member of the list, another returns the second member, and so on.

There are three ways to combine these building blocks:

1. Composition: one function can call another as a subroutine (e.g., the successor function is applied to the result of the zero function).
2. Recursion: the functions can be combined, in effect, to construct a for-loop, which iterates a certain operation *for* a given number of times.
3. Minimization: the functions can be combined, in effect, to construct a while-loop, which carries out a certain operation *while* a particular condition remains true.

To give a simple example, we can define a function that counts the number of items in a list:

Length (list) =
If list is empty then 0
Otherwise 1 + (length(tail list))

The first clause of the definition says that if the list is empty, that is, contains nothing, then its length is 0. The second clause says that otherwise we compute the successor of the length of the tail of the list. The tail of a list is the result of chopping off its first item, and the function is constructed from the set of identity functions. The second clause of the definition seems strange because, in defining length, we use length itself. The circularity is not vicious, but virtuous: it is the essence of recursion. To see how it works, let us consider what happens if we compute the length of the list, (a b c). The recursive line in the definition tells us that:

length(a b c)

equals:

(1 + (length (b c)))

which, using the recursive line again, equals:

(1 + (1 + (length (c)))))

which, using the recursive line again, equals:

(1 + (1 + (1 + (length( )))))

Each time we use the recursive line, we repeat a loop in which we cut off the head of the list and add 1 to the expression. Once these iterations reduce the list to null, as they have now done, the first line in the definition applies, and it returns the value, 0. Hence, we can now repeatedly apply the successor function to compute the value:

(1 + (1 + (1 + 0))) = 3

Thus, length can be computed recursively in terms of the successor and zero functions.

Similar recursive formulations allow us to define addition, multiplication, and other functions of the utmost complexity. Once a function has been constructed from the existing building blocks, it can enter into the construction of further functions, and so on indefinitely. According to a well-known thesis, sometimes known as Church's thesis (after the logician Alonzo Church, who proposed it in 1936), any computation whatsoever can be carried out by the appropriate procedure defined by recursive functions. The thesis cannot be proved true, because it is way of making explicit the purely intuitive notion of computation. It would have been proved false, however, if anyone had discovered a method of computation lying outside the recursive functions.

Concept Learning: The Analogy with Recursive Functions

Philosophers have sometimes argued — or appeared to argue, which in philosophy is perhaps the same thing — for a strong doctrine of innate ideas. No significant learning of new concepts occurs during the lifetime of an individual, according to Jerry Fodor (1980), because the learning of concepts is impossible. Fodor's argument can be summarized as follows:

> Consider a child who has mastered one conceptual domain, say, the propositional connectives, *and, or,* and *not,* and now ask yourself how this child could make the transition to a more powerful domain, such as the predicate calculus, which contains the quantifiers *any* and *some.* There is no way for the

child to represent the meaning of the quantifiers because the only concepts available to the child are those of the connectives. If the meaning of a concept cannot be represented, then the concept cannot be learned. Hence, the child cannot learn the quantifiers. The argument is quite general, and leads ineluctably to the conclusion that all concepts are innate.

Fodor allowed that ad hoc concepts—those of the sort that I discussed in the first half of the chapter—could be induced; his argument applies to their constituents, roughly speaking, to concepts at the level of words, but are all such concepts innate? No one knows for certain, but Fodor's argument can be rebutted (see Johnson-Laird, 1983, chap. 6). I summarize the rebuttal here, but my main purpose is to prepare the ground for an account of the minimum that has to be innate for concepts to be learnable.

Any argument that purports to show that concepts cannot be learned is in danger of proving too much, namely, that they cannot be innate, either. The danger arises because innate concepts must be the result of evolution, and evolution is analogous to learning. The neo-Darwinian process shuffles genes and selects the fittest individuals from the resulting population. These individuals then provide the genes for the next iteration of the process. Evolution is the original recursive process, and it can, indeed, be modeled computationally. The resulting program, as I show in chapter 3, is a learning machine. Hence, any argument to the effect that concepts cannot be learned is likely to show that they could not have been generated by a neo-Darwinian process, either. The strong argument also runs into another difficulty. Concepts can be used to construct new thoughts, which in turn can be used to construct new concepts, and so on ad infinitum. Infinitely many concepts are, therefore, potentially available to human beings. Genetic endowment is finite, however, so not all concepts can be innate. Some *are* acquired, and indeed you may have learned the concept of araeostyle from reading this chapter. It might be deemed to be an ad hoc concept rather than a concept proper, but if so, we need a principled way to distinguish between proper concepts and ad hoc concepts. None exists, as yet.

I can pinpoint the flaw in the strong argument against the learning of concepts by replaying the argument in terms of the development of a set of functions:

The process begins with the minimal apparatus of recursive functions. At this stage, the system is able to compute the successor, zero, and identity functions. It cannot compute the length of a list, addition, or any other of the higher arithmetical functions. The key step in the argument is the claim that the system cannot represent the length function because the only concepts available to it are those of the zero, successor, and identity functions, and if the system cannot represent a function, then it cannot learn the function. Hence, it cannot learn the length function or any other new functions.

The key step in the argument is wrong. The system has only the primitive functions, but it does not follow that it cannot represent the length function. On the contrary, it can do so using a recursive definition. Likewise, a child who has explicitly mastered only the sentential connectives may nevertheless have a powerful enough conceptual system to represent the meaning of the quantifiers, and so acquire them. In sum, the strong argument fails because it overlooks the distinction between current concepts and the computational power of the conceptual system. Concepts can be learned in principle. We can now consider the nature of concepts and how they are acquired in practice.

CONCEPTS: A THEORY AT THE COMPUTATIONAL LEVEL

On What There Is and How One Knows It

It is instructive to think for a moment about how and why we might equip a machine with a conceptual system. A machine that is able to classify objects can build up knowledge about their properties and behaviors, and this knowledge will enable it to make predictions about them. It is advantageous to learn that certain animals, artifacts, and natural events are dangerous; it is advantageous to learn that other entities are useful. The machine therefore needs to represent classes of entities in a way that will enable it to identify them, to learn about them, and to draw inferences about them. The visual recognition of objects calls for a catalogue of their three-dimensional shapes and a method of matching the representation of a particular view of a particular object with the appropriate model in the catalogue (Marr, 1982). The recognition of novel objects, particularly artifacts, often calls for identifying their potential function. What we need to consider is the ontology of daily life (i.e., the different sorts of things for which there are concepts) and the epistemology of concepts (i.e., the different sorts of knowledge embodied in concepts).

Three principal varieties of concept occur in the ontology of everyday life:

- Entities, which are either substances or discrete, countable things.
- Properties of entities.
- Relations among entities.

Because human beings categorize in order to draw consequences, they can do so only if otherwise distinct things support such inferences. The strongest possibility is that the world divides up into classes based on essential components that support necessary conclusions. The Empiricists, accordingly, supposed that concepts depend on common elements, and this idea underlies the inductive machines that I discussed earlier. Some concepts are indeed *analytic,* in that they have necessary and sufficient conditions. A triangle, for example, is a plane figure formed by joining three non-colinear points by straight lines, and any figure that meets this definition is a triangle. Likewise, an aunt is a sister of a parent, and anyone who meets this definition is an aunt. Some philosophers, such as Quine (1953), doubt the existence of any genuine analytic concepts, but these skeptics might concede that technical terms can be defined with necessary and sufficient conditions. The very notion of *analytic* seems itself to be such a technical term!

A weaker possibility is evinced by *natural kinds*: those natural objects, substances, properties, and relations—such as dogs, water, alive, and seeing—that cannot be categorized according to a set of necessary and sufficient conditions. It is easy to slip into the point of view that these concepts depend either on a "central tendency" of a set of attributes, or on a representation of a set of exemplars (see Estes, 1986; Kemler Nelson, 1984). Edelman (1987, p. 30) similarly argued for statistical combinations of attributes, or exemplars, because he located the origin of concepts in somatic selection from among huge numbers of variants of neural circuits, but what would be the purpose of classifying instances in such ways, and how would such classifications have arisen? You need to know what to count as a dog, before you can carry out a statistical survey of dogs to assess what proportion of them, say, have fur, or before you can store exemplars of them. An analogous difficulty arises from Rosch's (1977) theory that a prototype is a concrete image of a typical member of the concept. An image is a two-dimensional entity, and it is not obvious how it could be used to identify three-dimensional objects, or how it could be used to recognize atypical exemplars as instances of a concept. A chihuahua is a dog even though it is remote from the prototype.

Our concepts of dogs, water, alive, seeing, and other natural kinds approximate reality (we hope). Their true nature is unknown. Thus, the breeding of a new sort of dog, the discovery of a new sort of water, or the corroboration of a revolutionary scientific theory, might force us to revise our theory. We rely on experts—scientists, typically—for the richest theories; we, however, tend to have only incomplete or rudimentary theories (Putnam, 1975). We have a catalogue of the shapes, textures, and other perceptual properties of natural kinds to enable us to recognize their members, and perhaps some knowledge of how they fit together in the natural scheme of things (e.g., their behavior, habitat, and origins).

The theory of a natural kind groups its properties into three sorts: those, if any, that are necessary; those that normal instances have by default (i.e., that can be taken for granted unless there is evidence to the contrary, Minsky, 1975); and those peripheral properties that vary more or less freely from one instance to another, although the theory may include information about their variability from one instance to another, a factor that biases judgment (Nisbett, Krantz, Jepson, & Kunda, 1983). The resulting concept allows a considerable economy in perception, thought, and communication. Once an entity has been identified, it is necessary to pay attention only to its abnormal properties, and perhaps to the values of some of its peripheral attributes. Its normal values can be inferred from the theory by default, unless evidence exists to the contrary. Indeed, the way to identify that a concept is genuinely prototypical is not to show that it gives rise to "typicality" effects in judgments of membership—even concepts with necessary conditions can do so (Armstrong, L.R. Gleitman, & H. Gleitman, 1983)—but to show that it supports inferences by default. The concept of dog is prototypical because one infers by default that a dog has four legs, a tail, and so on. The prototypical dog fits a model based on the concept and on all of its necessary and default values.

Another class of concepts is exemplified by games, chairs, and melodies. They are neither analytic nor based on empirical theories. They have, instead, what might be termed a *constructive* foundation, that is, they have no objective correlates in the physical world. No scientific theory postulates an analysis of what counts as a game or a chair or a melody. Instead, these entities depend on mental constructs that are imposed upon the world by their use in the design of artifacts. Typically, they concern function rather than intrinsic structure. What counts as a melody is not determined by the physical structure of real entities, but by our conception of certain musical relations. One culture's melody is another's noise.

From an analysis of a significant fragment of the English lexicon, George Miller and I concluded that lexical meanings are organized into semantic fields (Miller & Johnson-Laird, 1976). Underlying such a semantic field is a conceptual core, a theory-like structure that integrates the different concepts in the semantic field around one or two core concepts, such as color, kinship, motion, possession, and perception. These concepts are interrelated by concepts that occur in many fields, including concepts of space, time, possibility, and permissibility. The theory of a conceptual core underlies the paramount fact that concepts are not isolated mental tokens. They are organized taxonomically by the conceptual relations into which they enter. These taxonomies enable us to categorize things without having to be equipped with precise concepts. Analytic concepts are precise, but natural kinds and constructed entities are not, so the boundaries between their instances cannot be mapped with absolute precision. These concepts have to allow for future states of affairs. Our notions of flora, fauna, and artifacts have to anticipate entities that we have not yet encountered or that will exist only in the future. It would be a massive undertaking to specify concepts that were both precise and open to the future, and their acquisition would be likely to defeat any ordinary individual.

The human conceptual system has evolved so that it is easy to acquire, open to the future, and simple to use. Concepts are often incomplete, and they incorporate default values. The boundaries of such a concept's extension — the entities that count as its instances — are fixed, not just by the information in the mental specification of the concept, but by the particular taxonomy into which the concept enters. Whether something is to count as a table depends on its relation to our concepts of tables, desks, bureaus, and other notions in the same conceptual field. The advantage of this principle of classification is that it yields vagueness in extensions, and so we are not forced to be precise in cases where we are ignorant.

Where greater precision is needed, we can refine our concepts. The conceptual system is indeed recursive: properties and relations can have properties, relations can enter into relations, and so on, in increasingly complicated ways that culminate both in more precise properties and in concepts corresponding to events, states of affairs, processes, and other complex interrelations.

In summary, the analysis of concepts as sets of necessary and sufficient conditions, and the alternative analysis in terms of prototypes, are both overgeneralized inductions. Concepts are heterogeneous. They fall into three main categories (Johnson-Laird, 1983; Keil, 1991):

1. Analytic concepts that have necessary and sufficient conditions by intention, and that concern logical, philosophical, and mathematical notions together with those of such "closed worlds" as kinship.
2. Natural concepts that depend on science for their discovery, but that otherwise depend on everyday theories that are incomplete and contain default values.
3. Constructive concepts that have a conventional or deontic basis, which may differ from one culture to another.

The system of concepts is summarized in Table 3 with examples of each of the main varieties in each of the main ontological categories: entities, properties, and relations.

One further dimension is crucial for concepts. It is necessary to keep track of their epistemic status. A concept may represent something that is actual, such as a dog; something that is a possibility, such as a yeti; something that is counterfactual — that was once thought to be possible but is now known not to exist — such as polywater; or something that is impossible, such as clean dirt. What is needed is a theory that integrates

TABLE 3.
Some Examples Illustrating the Ontological and Epistemological Classification
of Concepts

	The epistemological dimension		
	Analytical concepts	Natural concepts	Constructive concepts
The ontological dimension: Entities			
Objects	triangle	dog	table
Substances	space	water	food
Properties	straight	alive	expensive
Relations	causes	sees	owns

necessary conditions and defaults, just as the system of deductive reasoning in chapter 1 integrated valid deduction and non-monotonic reasoning.

The Nature of Primitive Concepts: A Theory of Subconcepts

Concepts, I have argued, enable you to envisage instances of entities, properties, and relations. You can construct mental models on the basis of the information they contain. They also enable you, at least in principle, to identify instances, although you may depend on taxonomic information and on expert testimony for a definitive identification. In addition, they enable you to make inferences about their instances (by virtue of having categorized them). These inferences concern such matters as the provenance of an entity, its behavior, its internal structure, its use, and its relations to instances of other concepts. Any particular piece of information may serve more than one of these functions, but a proper grasp of a concept calls for at least some information that serves to envisage, to identify, and to make inferences. I now outline a new theory of the constituents of concepts that offers an explanation of how concepts are mentally represented in a way that meets these various purposes.

Because some concepts, such as araeostyle, are learned from others, some concepts must be more basic than others. The nature of the more basic concepts, however, has proved to be highly problematical. For example, the meaning of a concept, such as:

woman

might be broken down into the following sort of constituent concepts (Katz & Fodor, 1963):

human & adult & female

which would be recovered whenever the word is understood. Yet, attempts to corroborate such decompositions into constituents have failed (Fodor, Fodor, & Garrett, 1975; Johnson-Laird, 1983, chap. 10; Kintsch, 1974).

One response to such failures might be to argue that there are no constant concepts. Barsalou (1987) asserted: "invariant representations of categories do not exist in human cognitive systems." He based his claim on the variability of human performance, particularly with ad hoc concepts, such as "ways to escape being killed by the Mafia." But, if concepts were in eternal flux, then the claim to that effect would itself be in flux, too. It would lie outside the scope of empirical investigation because it would have no stable meaning. Much thinking indeed depends on the construction of instances of ad hoc concepts in working memory, but the compositional understanding of a concept, such as:

ways to escape being killed by the Mafia

depends on stable notions in long-term memory. To claim that people envisage different instances of the same category on different occasions makes sense only if there is something that counts as the *same* category. Not all is flux, and concepts are relatively stable. What fluctuates are instances of them that are called to mind, and the referential border between one concept and another.

Another response to the lack of evidence for decomposition is to argue that there are no basic concepts. That is, all concepts are basic because words stand in a one-to-one relation with the conceptual tokens of the language of thought (Fodor, 1975; J.D. Fodor et al., 1975; Kintsch, 1974). This view fails to square with the phenomena of comprehension. Suppose I describe to you a state of affairs, such as:

The circle is on the right of the triangle.

You can envisage this situation. You can check whether the assertion is true in certain circumstances, and you can use it to make a deduction. The mere translation of the sentence into a mental language with tokens for each concept:

(ON-RIGHT-OF CIRCLE TRIANGLE)

or a translation into a semantic network (e.g., Quillian, 1968), does not account for these abilities. When you envisage the situation, you do not imagine linguistic entities in a syntactic organization. If ON-RIGHT-OF were the most basic representation of the relation, then you could never verify the assertion, because such a representation contains no information enabling you to determine what counts as satisfying the relation. Likewise, as we saw in chapter 1, the evidence goes against linguistic theories of deduction. It follows that there must be some more fundamental machinery that enables you to envisage the circle on the right of the triangle, to grasp the truth conditions of the assertion, and to make deductions from it.

The solution to this problem is to posit a set of ultimate conceptual primitives, or *subconcepts,* that form the mental representation of concepts. They are the building blocks needed to construct thoughts—that is, propositions about real or imaginary situations—and to construct models that make explicit particular instances of those thoughts. To see that the circle is on the right of the triangle is to construct a perceptual model of the situation. To understand that the circle is on the right of the triangle is to assemble a proposition that can be used to construct a model of the situation, although such a model is more schematic and less vivid than a perceptual one. Certain subconcepts underlie the construction of perceptual models: they include subconcepts for colors, shapes, and textures in the case of vision, and subconcepts for sounds, tastes, and odors in the case of other modalities (G.A. Miller & Johnson-Laird, 1976). Other subconcepts relate to the internal milieu—bodily and emotional states; and still others to mental states—subconcepts for possibility, permissibility, and intentionality.

As an illustration of the theory of subconcepts, I consider its implementation in the program for spatial reasoning that I mentioned in the previous chapter. The program constructs three-dimensional models on the basis of verbal assertions. It has a lexicon in which each word has a subconceptual analysis of its meaning, and it has a grammar in which each rule has a corresponding semantic principle for forming subconceptual combinations, principles that are analogous to the methods of combining recursive functions. As the program parses a sentence, it uses these subconceptual combinations to assemble a representation of the sentence's meaning. This *propositional representation* is then used by other procedures to construct a model of a particular situation described by the sentence.

Given a noun-phrase such as *the circle,* the program uses the subconcept underlying *circle* to set up a simple model:

○

Given the assertion:

The circle is on the right of the triangle.

the parsing process combines the subconcepts underlying the words in the sentence to yield the following result, which is the propositional representation of the meaning of the sentence:

((1 0 0)(◯)(△))

The meaning of the relation x *on the right of* y is a subconcept that consists of set of values for incrementing the values of Cartesian coordinates:

The 1 indicates that x should be located by incrementing y's value on the left–right dimension while holding y's values on the front–back and up–down dimensions constant, that is, by adding 0s to them.

What the program does with the propositional representation of the meaning of a sentence depends on context. If the assertion is the first in a discourse, the program uses the representation to construct a complete model within a minimal spatial array:

Otherwise, depending on the current set of models, the program uses the propositional representation to add an entity to a model, to combine two previously separate models, to make a valid deduction, or to make a non-monotonic inference. For example, the program can make a transitive deduction, such as:

>   The circle is on the right of the triangle.
>   The cross is on the right of the circle.
> ∴ The cross in on the right of the triangle.

without relying on any explicit statement of transitivity. It uses the subconcepts for *on the right of* to construct the model:

It verifies the conclusion in the model, and is unable to find an alternative model of the premises in which the conclusion is false. In summary, subconcepts combine to form propositional representations that can be used by several different procedures for constructing and manipulating models.

The concept of *on the right of* is part of a system based on the same underlying set of subconcepts:

on the right of	1	0	0
on the left of	−1	0	0
in front of	0	1	0
behind	0	−1	0
above	0	0	1
below	0	0	−1

This subconceptual system is an idealized taxonomy. In the real world, objects do not have to be perfectly aligned, and so a judgment of the relation between them may compare their actual coordinates with alternative possibilities in the taxonomy. The evidence suggests that human reasoners represent spatial relations in an analogous way (Johnson-Laird & Byrne, 1991). That is to say, their representation of spatial relations, such as *on the right of,* enables them to construct and manipulate spatial models. Indeed, the procedures for manipulating models probably exist prior to the mastery of any particular spatial relation and can be used to acquire new high-level concepts. For example, one might acquire the relation represented in the program by (1 0 1): *diagonally up and to the right.* Repeated encounters with such a relation in spatial models, if it played an important part in spatial thinking, could lead ultimately to the abstraction of the relation as a new concept. The human spatial system may not use coordinates, but it must use some analogous subconceptual system to capture truth conditions; otherwise, human reasoners could neither envisage situations nor determine whether assertions are true or false. Subconcepts, however, lie outside conscious awareness and are not available for inspection. They are ineffable, that is, not necessarily expressible in the language of everyday discourse. Thus, if the coordinate solution is on the right lines, then it is used by English speakers who have no conscious knowledge of coordinate systems and no immediately available language in which to talk about them. The discovery of human subconcepts is a matter for scientific investigation.

The theory is intended to apply to concepts as a whole. Analytic concepts, such as triangles and squares, are constructed from spatial subconcepts. Concepts of natural kinds and artifacts are complex constructions that depend, in part, on subconcepts that specify default values. When all the defaults are used to construct a model, then the result is a model of the prototypical case — that is, an instantiation of the concept with all its default values — but the subconcept can also be used to construct models of other, more unusual, instantiations, such as three-legged dogs, stripeless tigers, and green carnations. One crucial point is that the subconcepts in a conceptual representation suffice for the construction of mental models, and thus play a part in relating concepts to the world, but they alone may not determine the reference of terms. The world can present you with entities that are difficult or impossible to identify. You can construct a perceptual model of such entities, but you run into trouble in identifying them. Your judgment of the extension of a concept may depend on the relative "distance" of an entity from competing concepts in the same taxonomy.

The Nature of Subconceptual Combinations

Concepts can enter into a variety of combinations. One concept can represent a property of another, one concept can be included in another and so form a hierarchy of class inclusion, one concept may correspond to part of an object captured by another concept and so form a part–whole hierarchy, and one concept can be part of a contrastive set of concepts. The most general case is of a relational concept that interrelates two other concepts. A typical case occurs when a spatial relation, such as *on the right of,* interrelates instances of two concepts. What the system of subconceptual combination has to provide is both the machinery that allows the appropriate assembly of these constituents—the syntax of conceptual combination—and the machinery that allows the resulting combination to receive its correct interpretation—the compositional interpretation of subconceptual combinations.

This machinery serves several functions. It plays a part in the everyday comprehension of assertions and their corresponding ad hoc concepts, such as buildings with equidistant columns; it enables permanent concepts to be constructed out of simpler concepts; and it provides the framework that organizes the interrelations among concepts in an economical way by forming such interrelations as: *instance of, part of, opposite of*— an intuition that lies behind the notion of semantic networks (Collins & Quillian, 1969; Quillian, 1968). In other words, the principles of subconceptual combination underlie both the organization of concepts and their composition into more complex concepts.

The syntax of conceptual combination is unknown. Since Frege's (1879/1967) invention of the predicate calculus, it has been natural to assume that the "language of thought" has a predicate–argument structure like that of the predicate calculus, but in fact we do not even know whether the mental language is sequentially organized, as opposed, say, to organized in several dimensions. What we can be more certain about is the semantics of subconceptual combinations. The procedure for interpreting a relation and its arguments must be able to assemble the concepts corresponding to the arguments and to compose them with the interpretation of the relation. I illustrated this process of composition earlier in describing the representation of spatial relations. Its key component is analogous to the notion of one procedure calling others as subprocedures (i.e., "composition" in the language of recursive function theory). Because relations tend to place constraints on the entities they relate, the process of combination has to ensure that these constraints are satisfied. Linguists used to refer to these constraints as "selectional restrictions," but their origin is in the conceptual system rather than in the language (Miller & Johnson-Laird, 1976, sec. 5.1.5; Smith, 1988).

To demonstrate the application of the subconceptual theory, I now consider two important conceptual relations: the relation of causation and the relation of ownership. Causation is a relation that occurs in nearly all semantic fields. Ownership is a relation that underlies an entire semantic field, and it is an example of an everyday concept that depends on a recursive form of conceptual combination.

The Concept of Causation

In the everyday theory of causation, every event has a cause, and the cause occurs prior to its effect—often immediately prior to it and in physical contiguity to it (Miller & Johnson-Laird, 1976, sec. 6.3; Lewis, 1986). Hence, if an action on an object is followed at once by a change in the object, then human reasoners make the plausible induction that the action caused the change. When they judge the likelihood of an event, they often rely on the *representativeness* heuristic: they assess whether the event is "similar in its essential properties to its parent population," and "reflects the salient features of the process by which it is generated" (Kahneman & Tversky, 1972). Hence, they tend to assume that outcomes resemble their causes.

The everyday theory takes causation as a primitive unanalyzed notion. Theorists often either make the same assumption or analyze the concept in terms of postulates such as:

probability (effect/cause) > probability (effect/$\neg$ cause)

as proposed by Cheng and Novick (1991). According to the subconceptual theory, the construction of causal models depends on subconcepts, and three sets of subconcepts appear to be required: those for temporal relations, those for negation, and those for epistemic states (facts, possibilities, counterfactual states, and impossibilities). These sets of subconcepts underlie a taxonomy of causal relations. To believe that situations of a class, A, cause those of a class, B, is to believe that it is not physically possible for an A to occur without a B occurring. The general claim corresponds to the following set of initial models:

Possibilities: [A]   B
                                    · · ·

where the onset of A occurs prior to the onset of B, and the models represent physical possibilities. These models can be fleshed out explicitly to represent either the notion of a necessary and sufficient cause:

Possibilities: A   B
                   $\neg$A $\neg$B

or the weaker notion of a sufficient cause:

Possibilities: A   B
                   $\neg$A   B
                   $\neg$A $\neg$B

The subconceptual system underlies six classes of causal relation that correspond to strong or weak notions of causing, enabling, and preventing. Table 4 shows the initial models for each of them. The same relations may occur among models that represent situations that are permissible or situations that represent logical possibilities. Hence, there are the parallel relations in three domains:

   Physical domains: Causes – Prevents – Enables
   Deontic domains: Obligates – Prohibits – Allows
   Logical domains: Implies – Contradicts – Coheres

Causal relations may also be about specific events; in this case, they can be expressed either by simple indicative assertions of the form:

A caused B.

TABLE 4.
The Six Classes of Causal Relation and Their Initial Mental Models, Where Each Model Represents a Possible Situation, and the Square Parentheses Indicate That a State Has Been Exhaustively Represented in a Model

A causes B (strong relation)	A prevents B (strong relation)
[A] [B]	[A] [$\neg$ B]
· · ·	· · ·
A causes B (weak relation)	A prevents B (weak relation)
[A] B	[A] $\neg$ B
· · ·	· · ·
A allows B	A allows not B
A [B]	A [$\neg$ B]
· · ·	· · ·

or by counterfactual conditionals of the form:

If A hadn't happened then B wouldn't have happened.

Such a counterfactual is normally interpreted in the following way:

Fact: A   B
Counterfactual: $\neg$A $\neg$B

The causal interpretation of a particular sequence of events according to this analysis must depend on the background knowledge of a general causal relation, because the events themselves will be consistent with more than one interpretation. If you observe, for example, a patient who loses consciousness after an injection, then your causal interpretation of the events will depend on your background knowledge. In the case that the injection is an anaesthetic, then you are likely to construct the models:

Fact: i   l
Counterfactual: $\neg$i $\neg$l

which you can describe in the following words:

If the patient hadn't been injected then he wouldn't have lost consciousness.

In the case that the injection was insulin given too late to a diabetic, then you are likely to construct the models:

Fact: i   l
Counterfactual: [$\neg$ i]   l
                          . . .

which you can describe in the following words:

If the patient hadn't been injected, then he would have lost consciousness anyway.

The implicit counterfactual model allows that the injection might have prevented the loss of consciousness: i $\neg$l.

In summary, the subconcepts underlying the various causal relations treat them, not as mere correlations between events, but as relations between what is possible and what is impossible in the domain of physical possibilities. Of course, one can also conceive of probable causes, but they can be treated by embedding causal models of the sort I have described within a framework of probabilities.

The Concept of Ownership

Like causation, the concept of ownership is often treated by theorists and lay people as irreducible, but in fact it is based on subconcepts (Miller & Johnson-Laird, 1976, sect. 7.2). Where an individual owns an object, the normal relation of ownership depends on the following conceptual combinations:

1. It is is permissible for the individual to use the object, and it is not permissible for others to prevent the individual from using the object.
2. It is permissible for the individual to give others permission to use the object; otherwise, it is not permissible for them to use it.

Finally, but rarely for an everyday concept, there is a conceptual combination that is recursive. If one individual transfers ownership of an object to another, then it is not just the object that is transferred but also the right to transfer ownership to yet another individual, who also has the right to transfer it, and so on. Hence, this condition calls for a recursive combination:

3. If an individual owns an object, then it is permissible for the individual to act so as to cause someone else to own the object.

These three principles constitute the theory at the conceptual core of ownership. They are based, in turn, on the subconcepts that underlie three important conceptual taxonomies: the deontic domain (i.e., permission), the causal domain (i.e., cause), and the domain of intentional action (i.e., act). In an intentional act, the actor has a goal in mind, such as a change in ownership, realizes that a certain action will bring about this goal, and then, in the light of this knowledge, carries out the action in order to achieve the goal. Intention, on this account, is more than goal-directed behavior: it depends recursively on a conscious realization that one can act intentionally (Johnson-Laird, 1983, chap. 16).

The three principles of ownership are also relevant to other concepts in the same taxonomy. Thus, the first principle is central to the notion of borrowing an object. If the second principle is dropped, the analysis captures the notion of exclusive use. If the final recursive principle is dropped, the analysis captures the notion of nontransferable property (e.g., the hiring of certain objects).

The key point about the concepts of ownership and causation is that they normally function as quasi-primitives. They can be represented in mental models by simple tokens that do not make explicit their underlying subconcepts. Subconcepts are called upon only when it is necessary to evaluate the truth value of propositions or to make inferences that hinge on the subconcepts, that is, to build more explicit models. Granted the concept of ownership, the proposition that Pat (p) gave Evelyn (e) a book (b) can be represented by a sequence of mental models of states of affairs at different times, t and t′:

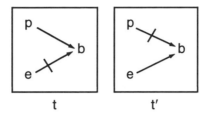

t   t′

The arrow represents ownership, and the barred arrow represents its negation. What the two models do not represent is that the change of state was caused by an intentional action: Pat, for example, put the book into Evelyn's hands and said: "Here's a present for you." Given the state of affairs in the model at t, such an action, A, caused the state of affairs represented in the model at t′. The causal relation is accordingly captured in the following models:

Fact:	model at t	A	model at t′
Counterfactual:	model at t	¬A	¬model at t′

Ownership is a constructive concept. One cannot observe the relation perceptually, but only evidence that bears upon it, such as the acts that bring about a change in ownership. It is a concept that depends on deontic subconcepts and on the regulative conventions of society. They fix the sorts of individuals that can own property, the sorts of entities that can be property, and the modes of conveyance and inheritance. They allow the normal constitutive conventions to be overruled, as when one restrains an individual who is using a possession in a dangerous way. These conventions differ from one society and epoch to another. They place constraints on the sorts of entities between which the relation can hold. Thus, an owner is of necessity a person or group, and is assumed by default to be an adult. The entities that can be owned range from artifacts to real estate. Ownership of a mountain is a possibility, but not perhaps ownership of a cloud.

CONCEPTS AND THE DESIGN OF THE HUMAN INDUCTIVE SYSTEM

The Innate Components of Induction

Although studies in psychology and artificial intelligence have been revealing, no one has described a feasible program for human induction. What I want to consider here are some of the design characteristics that any plausible theory must embody. If nothing else, these characteristics show why no existing program is adequate for human induction. The agenda is set by the apparatus of recursive functions. I begin with the innate basis of concepts.

There are many competing theories about the basis of concepts. At the two extremes are Empiricism and Nativism. Empiricists claim that the innate mechanisms of perception furnish the mind with various perceptual properties, and innately based judgments of similarity allow the child to construct concepts (e.g., Quine, 1960). This basis, however, is inadequate. It fails to account for those concepts — from deontic notions to quantifiers — that have no grounding in perception. Nativists claim that all concepts, apart from those constructed on an ad hoc basis, are innate. This view, too, as we have seen, is inadequate. Between the two extremes lie various proposals about innate "theories." Carey (1985) argued that children are equipped with one or two primal theories: a naive theory of behavior and a naive theory of the mechanics of physical objects. Keil (1991) has defended a pluralistic view in which the child is innately equipped with a more diverse set of theories. Others argue that new concepts are formed by a process of enrichment from core principles that are constant; that is, new concepts are derived from old by processes of inductive generalization (Spelke, 1991). The most radical proposal is that children's concepts pass through revolutionary changes akin to those that occur in science (Piaget & Inhelder, 1969). Such developments, as Carey (1991) emphasized, imply that children's concepts may be incommensurable with those of adults, and that ". . . new concepts may arise that are not definable in terms of concepts already held". Carey has not proposed any mechanism for the development of concepts, although she repudiates the Piagetian account. I return to this problem and the creation of novel concepts in chapter 3.

The theory of subconcepts offers a different view about the acquisition of concepts. Subconcepts are part of the innate basis of thought. They are analogous to the primitives of recursive function theory, or to the instruction set of a computer's central processor. The instruction set, which has the power of recursive functions, is "wired in" to the processor. Computer programs written in high-level languages, such as LISP, are translated into the language that elicits these instructions by special programs known as *compilers*. When a high-level program has been compiled in this way, the resulting compilation is no longer available for high-level editing. Likewise, when you grasp a concept, such as *on the right of,* you neither decompose it into semantic constituents, nor merely translate it into a token in the language of thought; rather, you access its subconcepts and combine them with others in readiness to construct a model. To have a concept fully available to you is, therefore, to have an automatic and unconscious access to its subconcepts, which play their part in the construction of models. Everyday concepts are thus akin to instructions in a high-level programming language, but when you use them to think, you rely on their mental compilation into subconcepts. That is why subconcepts cannot normally be put into words in an individual's native language. Subconcepts are innate, universal, and ineffable.

This theory, unlike others, implies that there are three distinct sources of concepts. The first source is evolution. What must be genetically endowed for the learning of concepts and the induction of hypotheses are three basic components:

1. A set of subconcepts (analogous to the zero, successor, and identity functions). These subconcepts include those for entities, properties, and relations that apply to the perceptual world, to bodily states and emotions, and to mental domains including deontic and epistemic states (facts, possibilities, counterfactual states, impossibilities). They are the ultimate components out of which all inductions are constructed, and they are used in the construction and manipulation of mental models. Various analyses of concepts have been made from both a machine and human standpoint (Jackendoff, 1989; Miller & Johnson-Laird, 1976; Schank, 1975), but the difficulty of isolating a definitive set of subconcepts cannot be overestimated. It is of little use to define one concept, such as *woman,* in terms of other high-level concepts, such as *adult, human, female.* The concept must be analyzed in a way that will be useful for the construction of models of the world. What is needed is an analysis of the satisfaction conditions of our most basic ideas and their interrelations. These conditions enable us to envisage the world and in certain circumstances to verify our imaginings.

2. A set of methods for combining subconcepts and concepts, which includes composition and recursion, and perhaps minimization. The subconcepts and combinations act in concert to enable mental models to be constructed out of the ingredients that they supply.

3. A set of inductive mechanisms. It is these mechanisms that make possible the induction of concepts and conjectures.

The second source of concepts is knowledge by compilation. It depends on an inductive mechanism that assembles them (and their taxonomic interrelations) out of the set of innate subconcepts and combinations. Verbal instruction alone is no use here: there is no substitute for the construction of models of the world — its entities, properties, and relations. Ultimately, the repeated construction of models, as I suggested in the case of *diagonally up and to the right,* enables the relevant concept to be compiled into subconcepts.

Concepts constructed from subconcepts are heterogeneous: some have necessary and sufficient conditions; others are open-ended, and prototypical, and depend on default values. This heterogeneity has consequences for the mechanism that constructs new concepts. Those concepts with necessary and sufficient conditions might be induced by a variant of the method that builds decision trees, but this method runs into difficulties with concepts that depend on prototypes. They might be acquired by a program that constructs hierarchies of clusterings, in which instances are grouped together in ways that are not all or none (e.g., Gennari, Langley, and Fisher, 1990; Pearl, 1986). They might be acquired by a connectionist procedure that constructs a distributed representation (e.g., Hanson and Bauer, 1989; Hinton, 1986). In computer experiments, Quinlan (1990) has examined the learning of artificial prototypical concepts in which instances are classified according to their nearest neighbor in multidimensional space. Decision-tree programs, such as ID3, have problems in learning them: an impossible amount of data has to be presented for the system to learn correctly. They are easier for a connectionist program, which is good at combining many weak and noisy pieces of evidence. Conversely, where concepts depend on many subconcepts, but only one or two are needed to classify any instance (i.e., the relevance of one subconcept depends on the presence of others), then these concepts are hard for connectionist programs, but relatively easy for a decision-tree program.

Neither decision-tree nor connectionist programs correspond precisely to the required inductive mechanism. Its input, as I have argued, is a sequence of models, and its output is a heterogeneous set of concepts. This heterogeneity suggests that the mechanism builds up a hierarchy of defaults, exceptions, and necessary conditions. The mechanism must also be able to acquire concepts of objects, properties, relations, and quantification. Although there are proposals that are syntactically powerful enough to cope with these demands, no satisfactory program for inducing the corresponding concepts yet exists.

The third source of concepts is knowledge by composition. It constructs concepts and conjectures by composing them out of existing high-level concepts as a result of either description or acquaintance with instances. Hence, it comes into play only after some high-level concepts have been assembled out of subconcepts. Many machine programs are static in that they construct new concepts out of a fixed basic set that depends on the user's specification of the inductive problem (e.g., Mitchell, 1977). The human inductive mechanism, however, is evolutionary. It constructs new concepts from those that it has previously constructed, and, unlike most existing programs, it can construct novel concepts in order to frame an inductive hypothesis. It can also deploy compositional principles in the construction of concepts such as *araeostyle*. Existing programs can induce some compositional principles using explicitly structured representations (see Power & Longuet-Higgins, 1978; Selfridge, 1986), but they cannot yet induce such recursive concepts as *ownership*. Although connectionist systems can acquire rudimentary conceptual systems and rudimentary syntactic rules (e.g., Allen, 1988; Hanson & Kegl, 1987), they, too, are unable to emulate human competence.

Knowledge by composition, as in the case of *araeostyle,* can save time and trouble, but it is superficial. The shift from novice to expert in any conceptual domain appears to depend on knowledge by compilation. Only then can a concept be immediately used to construct models or to check that the concept is satisfied in a model constructed by perceptual or other means. Inductive hypotheses similarly depend on direct experience that adds information to models of the relevant domain.

The Case for Models in Induction

Theorists tend to think of induction as yielding conjectures that are linguistic generalizations. Hence, a major question has been to find the right language in which to represent concepts and conjectures. There has been much debate among the proponents of different mental languages, such as semantic networks, production systems, and versions of the predicate calculus. Yet, as I have argued, to think of the results of induction as linguistic representations may be a serious mistake. It may not do justice to human thinking. The purpose of induction is to make sense of the world, by enabling us to predict or to categorize more efficiently or, better still, to understand phenomena. The mind builds models, and the structure of models is the basis of human conceptions of the structure of the world. The product of induction may, therefore, be a model: either one that simulates the phenomenon (a descriptive induction) or one constructed from more elemental subconcepts (an explanatory induction). Models, in turn, can be used to formulate verbal generalizations.

One advantage of models is that the inductive mechanism for constructing conjectures and ad hoc concepts needs, in principle, only one operation of generalization: the addition of information to models. This operation is equivalent to quite diverse effects on linguistic conjectures. When it leads to the elimination of a model, it is equivalent to adding the negation of the description of that model to the current verbal hypothesis.

It can also have the effect of a *universal generalization,* which introduces a universal quantifier in place of an existential. And, it can have the effect of promoting an existential quantifier from inside to outside the scope of a universal quantifier, as in the transformation from:

Each of the symptoms is caused by a virus.

to:

A virus causes each of the symptoms.

Another advantage of models is that they embody knowledge in a way that naturally constrains inductive search. They maintain semantic information, they ensure internal consistency, and they are parsimonious because each entity is represented only once. They can also focus attention on the critical parts of the phenomena. An instructive example is provided by Novak's (1977) program for solving textbook problems in physics. It initially represents problems in a semantic network, but this representation contains too much information, so the program extracts from it a model of the situation that is used to identify the points where forces have to balance.

One final advantage of models is that they elucidate the clues about induction that have emerged from the psychological laboratory. Because of the limited processing capacity of working memory, models represent only certain information explicitly and the rest implicitly. One consequence is that people fall into error, and the evidence shows they make the same sorts of error in both deduction and induction. Thus, in deduction, they concentrate on what is explicit in their models, and so fail to make *modus tollens* or to carry out the selection task correctly (see chapter 1). In induction, they likewise focus on what is explicit in their models, and so seldom seek anything other than evidence that might corroborate their inductive hypotheses. They eschew negative instances, and encounter them only when they arise indirectly as a result of following up alternative hypotheses (e.g., Klayman & Ha, 1987; Wason, 1960, 1977). In deduction, they are markedly influenced by the way in which a problem is framed: what a model represents explicitly depends on what is explicitly asserted, and individuals have difficulty in fleshing out models completely (see, e.g., the difference between ordinary conditionals and those expressed with *only if,* which I discussed in chapter 1). In induction, there are equally marked effects of how a problem is framed (Hogarth, 1982). In both deduction and induction, reasoners are "satisficers": if they find a model that fits their available beliefs, they will tend not to search for others, and so may overlook the correct conclusion. Disjunctive alternatives are likewise particularly problematic. Reasoners have a natural preference to work with conjunction because it yields only a single model. The very preference of a "common element" analysis of concepts is just another manifestation of the same phenomenon. Finally, knowledge appears to play exactly the same part in both deduction and induction. It biases the process to yield more credible conclusions.

CONCLUSIONS

The principal contrast in induction is between specific and general inductions. Specific inductions are part of the normal process of comprehension: you flesh out your model of a discourse or the world with additional information that is automatically provided by your general knowledge. General inductions yield new models. They can also enrich your conceptual repertoire, generating either new ad hoc concepts or new concepts constructed from subconcepts. The human inductive mechanisms that carry out these tasks appear to embody five design characteristics that have yet to be implemented together in any inductive machine:

1. Their ultimate constituents are a set of subconcepts and conceptual combinations that are powerful enough to construct any mental model.
2. They can induce heterogeneous concepts of objects, properties, and relations. The repeated construction of models leads to the compilation of concepts that contain necessary subconcepts and default values.
3. They can construct novel ad hoc concepts, assembling them compositionally according to principles that generate recursively embedded structures.
4. They can add information to a model of a domain as a result of compilation or composition.
5. They are guided by constraints. They take into account available knowledge; they formulate the most specific generalizations consistent with the data and background knowledge; and, perhaps, they seek the simplest possible hypothesis consistent with the evidence.

The price of tractable induction is imperfection. We often concentrate on the triumphs of induction and the minor imperfections that yield clues to the nature of its mechanism. We overlook its catastrophes: the fads of pseudoscience, the nostrums of fringe medicine, the superstitions of daily life, and those instances of wishful thinking when, as at Chernobyl, individuals overlook the evidence that runs contrary to their deepest beliefs and desires. The origin of these errors is in the human inductive mechanism: its heuristics for satisficing are what students of other cultures refer to as "magical thinking." In addition, the pressure of working memory capacity often puts too much emphasis on what is explicitly represented in a model. Theorists, this theory argues, are bound to focus on what is explicitly represented in their models. The reader is invited to reflect on the recursive consequences of this claim for the present theory.

3 Creation

The French symbolist poet, Paul Valéry, was fascinated by the nature of creative processes. He rose before dawn each morning, and reflected upon the interior maneuvers of his own mind, and he recorded his thoughts in notebooks, which now fill a shelf in the Princeton University library, affording a unique record of the introspections of a great poet and thinker. On one occasion he met Einstein, and during their conversation asked him whether he, too, kept a notebook to record his thoughts. Einstein replied that he did not. He had a good idea so seldom, he explained, that he had no need to write it down in order to remember it. Indeed, some creators have just a few great ideas, others have many good ideas, but most of us have just a few bad ideas.

Valéry struggled all his life to unravel the riddle of creativity, but other artists have suggested that the gift may be lost if scrutinized too closely. Scientists sometimes have an analogous reaction. Creativity, they say, depends on unfathomable processes that are beyond the power of machines. Henri Poincaré (1929), a compatriot of Valéry's, expressed this attitude in the following characteristic passage:

> Now we have seen that mathematical work is not simply mechanical, that it could not be done by a machine, however perfect. It is not merely a question of applying rules, of making the most combinations possible according to certain fixed laws. The combinations so obtained would be exceedingly numerous, useless, and cumbersome. The true work of the inventor consists in choosing among these combinations so as to eliminate the useless ones or rather to avoid the trouble of making them, and the rules which must guide this choice are extremely fine and delicate. It is almost impossible to state

them precisely; they are felt rather than formulated. Under these conditions, how imagine a sieve capable of applying them mechanically?

Poincaré's skepticism can be translated into modern terms: creativity depends on processes that are not computable. It has also been recently advanced in these terms by another mathematician, Roger Penrose (1989). Creativity depends on consciousness, and consciousness, he claimed, is not a computable process. If he is right, then either there are mental processes that cannot be emulated by any form of computer or it will be necessary to revise Church's thesis that any effective procedure can be constructed using the apparatus of recursive functions (see chapter 2).

The only evidence for the Poincaré-Penrose hypothesis is its authors' intuitions. Hence, whether creativity is computable remains an open question. The sensible strategy is to assume that it is computable until one is forced to abandon this hypothesis. Whether a *theory* of creativity should be computable is, I hope, beyond question. We need good reasons to advance theories that take so much for granted that it is impossible to implement them in computer programs. Unless we try to frame a computable theory, we are in danger of producing that most pernicious intellectual artifact: a theory that cannot be properly understood by anyone other than its author.

My plan in this chapter is to present an initial analysis of creativity that lays out what has to be satisfied if a process is to be creative. It follows from this analysis that there are only three classes of computational processes that could be creative. It also follows that creativity can occur in lowly everyday thinking as well as at the highest levels of art and science. In order to examine this hypothesis, and to bring out the distinction between prosaic and profound imagination, the chapter describes a number of investigations, and in particular, studies of musical and scientific creativity.

WHAT IS CREATIVITY?

The Nature of the Computation

Several theorists have tried to cut creativity down to size by arguing that if psychology takes care of general cognitive processes, creativity will take care of itself:

> *Creating occurs when ordinary mental processes in an able person are marshaled by creative . . . intentions.*
>
> —Perkins (1981)

. . . Creativity is an automatic consequence of having the proper representation of concepts in a mind.

—Hofstadter (1982)

. . . Creative individuals possess no extraordinary characteristics—basically they do what we are all capable of doing.

—Weisberg (1986)

There is some truth in the idea, yet it is no accident that most of us are not great innovators. Creative processes do occur in daily life, but for an individual to develop them in just one domain of expertise demands an exceptional amount of work and even, perhaps, some innately determined mental capacities.

In an earlier analysis of creativity (Johnson-Laird, 1988a, 1988b), I framed a working definition that covers both highly original productions and the imaginative thoughts of daily life. This definition assumes that an act of creation yields a result with three essential properties:

1. The result is formed from existing elements, but in a combination that is novel for the individual and perhaps for society as a whole. It is not merely perceived or remembered.
2. It satisfies pre-existing criteria.
3. It is not constructed by rote or derived by some other simple deterministic procedure. The process allows for freedom of choice.

We need to distinguish between the induction and the creation of a new concept or idea. Induction increases the semantic information in a set of observations and background knowledge: it goes beyond them, but merely by adding semantic information. A new concept or explanatory theory, as I argued in the previous chapter, can yield semantic information that *overlaps* the information in the initial knowledge. That is, a process of thought may yield certain novel ideas that are unrelated to its starting point, that abandon certain observations or premises as erroneous, and that replace one set of concepts by another less misleading set. The new concepts, as we shall see, may even be incommensurable with the old ones. Processes that yield such results, in my view, should be deemed to be creative. Of course, nothing hinges on the use of the label. If you wish to refer to inductive processes as "creative," then you are welcome to do so. My point is that there is an important theoretical difference between induction and creation (in the senses in which I have defined them). Induction depends on generalization; creation cannot depend on generalization alone. It may yield a model that revolutionizes the way we think about the world. I will, therefore, add a further property to those that underlie the working definition of creativity:

4. The result of a creative process in the realm of ideas yields semantic information that overlaps the information in the initial knowledge.

In the course of the next few sections, I examine these four properties in more detail.

Novelty, Uniqueness, and Criteria

Most definitions of creativity emphasize that its results should be novel and unique (e.g., Reber, 1985). Of course, new ideas cannot be constructed out of nothing: mental elements must exist to provide the raw materials for even highly original works of art or science. Furthermore, according to the model theory, these elements, like all elements of thought, ultimately depend on innate subconcepts and subconceptual relations. Individuals who merely regurgitate existing ideas from memory or perception are hardly creative. The results must be new — at least for the individual creator. Hence, granted that both Newton and Leibniz independently invented the calculus, both of them demonstrated great originality. Society may reserve the highest awards for those who are first, but uniqueness is a matter of history, not psychology. What we need to understand are the mental processes underlying the creation of ideas, and so, if we exclude cases of indirect influence or downright plagiarism, we can put to one side the issue of uniqueness.

The products of a creative act lie within a set of criteria: anything that is not categorizable is not creative. Artists create stories and poems, sonatas and symphonies, paintings and sculptures. They work within the constraints of a genre and their own personal style. Scientists create laws and explanations, concepts and conjectures, observational instruments and experimental procedures. Unlike artists, they are governed by an additional constraint: their results should be true or useful, or both. They usually work within the constraints of a scientific paradigm that characterizes "normal science" (Kuhn, 1970). Both art and science appear to be extensions of the ordinary processes of everyday thinking, but expertise calls for grasping the constraints of the artistic genre or scientific paradigm in a special way that I attempt to elucidate further on.

In the arts, just occasionally, a revolutionary change occurs in a genre: Masaccio introduced human emotions into Renaissance painting; Schönberg abandoned tonality in music; Eliot introduced the technique of collage into poetry. In the sciences, just occasionally a revolutionary change occurs in paradigm: Galileo pioneered the experimental method; Darwin conceived species as the result of evolution by natural selection; Einstein abandoned absolute space and time. Even when a new art or science is created, it too lies within the bounds of criteria—not anything goes!—but it may face hostility from those who do not grasp its fundamentals.

Society and culture influence the creative process. They lead to the crystallization of artistic genres and scientific paradigms. These constraints are the consequences of previous creative processes. They are transmitted, often with modifications, from one generation to the next. The individual creator is not a closed system, but is directly influenced by teachers, mentors, and collaborators, who convey social and cultural values. The individual internalizes these values in order to create. This process enables the aesthetic values of a society to influence the individual's creative processes, which, in turn, may contribute to the values that are passed on to the next generation. The role of leadership has been stressed by Simonton (1984) in a striking historiometric study. He has shown, for example, that there are important relations between historical events—wars, social revolutions, and other such junctures—and creativity. He wrote: "When the most famous creators and leaders are under scrutiny the distinction between creativity and leadership vanishes because creativity becomes a variety of leadership." There are many examples, but there are also notable exceptions: geniuses, such as J.S. Bach, who had no school of followers; leaders, such as Francisco Franco, who exercised little imagination to take control of a society. The mind of a successful leader may work in different ways from the mind of a successful creator.

Non-Determinism

Imagination is more than imitation or calculation. If you multiply two numbers together, the result may be a number that you have never thought of before, yet your response is not creative—even if you get the answer wrong. Most people have the strong intuition that when they are doing something creative, such as making up a story for a child, alternative possibilities exist at many points in the process. If they could go back in time and re-live the experience (with no knowledge of their first effort), they might take a different route the second time around. They do not feel that as soon as they take the first step everything thereafter is fixed, as it would be in a deterministic process. Creativity does not seem to be deterministic.

In computational theory, a machine that can yield different outcomes from the same input and internal state is known as *non-deterministic* (Hopcroft & Ullman, 1979). A machine that always followed a principle in making a decision would be deterministic. A machine that followed no principle, or made a correct choice—if there were one—by means that defy explanation would be non-deterministic. Real computers are deterministic unless they have a loose connection in them, but they can easily be made to simulate non-determinism. One method borrows a technique from the casino in Monte Carlo and chooses at random, or at least in a pseudo-random way. If there is just one choice that is correct, then a machine can simulate non-determinism by exploring all choices until it discovers the correct one.

Imagine that a great jazz musician, such as Charlie Parker, is improvising. At each point there are several possible phrases that he might play, and a very much larger set of phrases that he would never play. The actual possibilities are musically appropriate, falling within the constraints of the genre and of Parker's style. What determines which particular phrase Parker plays? If you say that musical considerations always determine the choice — one phrase suggests another, for instance — then they must allow only one possible phrase at each point. Parker could improvise only as many solos as there are initial phrases, and we are back to determinism once again. This argument is quite general: the imaginative process of an artist or scientist is open, in that it is rarely so constrained that only one possibility can occur next. The creative individual has freedom of choice.

If Parker wanted to wake up his audience, he could deliberately play a sequence of wrong notes, a phrase that violates the harmonic and rhythmic conventions of the genre. He could deliberately choose to ignore the criteria of the music. During a normal performance, however, there is no time for a sequence of *intentional* decisions. A deliberate decision to ignore criteria lies outside normal creative practice, but it has been elevated to dogma by certain modern artists. Their slogan is, "The only genre is that there is no genre." Ever since the Dadaists, a vein of artistic thinking has existed that proclaims, "Anything goes," so composers, writers, painters, and choreographers, have experimented with random techniques. This device is freedom of choice at a meta-level: individuals can freely choose to let their decisions be made for them by external means, but the results are usually sifted by the exercise of artistic judgment. Purely random techniques are easy for machines. Without the exercise of judgment, however, they do not yield memorable works of art.

There are different ways to interpret a non-deterministic choice from within a set of possibilities. One interpretation is that the choice of, say, the particular phrase that Parker plays depends on some miniscule aspect of his mind, body, or environment. Such factors could include the beat of his pulse, the audience's response, or other events outside purely musical considerations. A causal explanation of how his choices are determined by such factors would amount to a deterministic theory, but we may never have such a theory. Creative processes are deterministic according to this interpretation, but, as the study of chaotic systems has revealed, a minute change in circumstances rapidly leads to major differences in outcome. Our ignorance forces us to model creativity non-deterministically.

Another interpretation of non-determinism is that the mind contains a mechanism for making arbitrary choices. People are poor at making genuinely random choices, but departures from true randomness do not count against the existence of such a mechanism. They imply only that the mind is not equipped with a random-number generator. Nevertheless, it can make an arbitrary decision from among a set of possibilities.

Still another interpretation is that quantum indeterminacies have a direct bearing on mental processes. This idea was originally proposed by the physicist Sir Arthur Eddington as a solution to the riddle of free will. Nothing could be less like freedom, however, than to be at the mercy of random quantum events. Free will is perhaps better interpreted as the meta-ability of choosing how to choose (Johnson-Laird, 1988b). More recently, Penrose (1989) has argued that a proper understanding of the brain's functioning calls for taking quantum events into account, but the inability of people to generate random choices suggests that if the brain is influenced by quantum indeterminacies, it cannot fully exploit them.

In summary, each choice in a normal act of creation is from among the possibilities specified by a set of criteria. The cumulative effect of the open nature of these possibilities permits an infinite number of potential creations, just as the rules of language permit an infinite number of different sentences. If the criteria allowed only one possibility at each step in the process, there would be only as many works of art, or scientific theories, as the number of different beginnings. Once started, the results of the process would be wholly determined. That, I submit, is an implausible basis for a theory of creation. An explanation of creativity is therefore forced to introduce non-determinism because it cannot account for how the choice among alternative possibilities is made.

THE COMPUTATIONAL ARCHITECTURE OF CREATIVITY

The Concept of Computational Power

If a machine is to be creative, then how powerful will it have to be? The question is instructive because certain forms of human creativity appear to depend on circumventing the restricted power of the mind. To grasp what is at stake, however, we need to investigate computational power.

The concept of computational power concerns *what* a machine can do rather than the efficiency of the operation. One machine is more powerful than another if it can carry out computations that are beyond the scope of the other. The weakest class of computational devices, *finite-state machines,* have only a finite number of distinct states but they are controlled by a set of instructions, which may be able to produce an infinite number of different outputs. For example, a machine for carrying out binary addition needs only two states — one for when a carry has occurred from the previous column, and one for when it has not occurred — and a set of instructions for adding pairs of binary digits in each of these two states. The critical feature of a finite-state machine is that it uses its states as a memory, and so it has only a finite memory for the intermediate results of computations.

Memory is the heart of computational power. The freer is the access to memory the greater is the power of a machine. The first significant step in power is to a *push-down automaton,* a finite-state machine equipped with a memory consisting of a stack onto which items can be placed. The stack is theoretically of unlimited depth, but it allows only a limited access to the items in memory. The machine has direct access only to the top-most item on the stack; so, whenever it puts something into memory it puts it on top of the stack. The first item into memory is accordingly the last item out. A finite-state machine without memory cannot carry out the computations needed to check that parentheses match in arithmetic expressions, such as: ((1 + 2) × (4 − 3)). With a stack, however, it can easily do so. It works along an expression from left to right; each time it encounters a left parenthesis, it puts it on the stack, and each time it encounters a right parenthesis, it removes the topmost item from the stack. A well-formed expression is one that starts and ends with nothing on the stack and that never calls for a symbol to be removed from an empty stack.

A finite-state machine that is allowed free access to memory is still more powerful. If the size of its memory is directly related to the length of the input expression, the machine is a *linear automaton.* If memory is freely accessible and unrestricted in size, then the resulting machine is equivalent in power to the full domain of recursive functions (see chapter 2). If Church's thesis is correct, such a machine can be programmed to carry out any computation whatsoever.

The input–output relations of any machine, even one that is non-deterministic, can be characterized by a set of rules, that is, by a grammar. As the machines increase in power, so the grammars must also increase in power. The "Chomsky hierarchy" arranges grammars in increasing power corresponding to machines of increasing power:

- Regular grammars for finite-state machines.
- Context-free grammars for push-down machines.
- Context-sensitive grammars for linear machines.

- Unrestricted transformational grammars for machines with random access memory.

Although a particular set of rules precisely characterizes the output of a machine, it does not follow that the machine is explicitly following these rules. There are many ways in which to carry out any computation — provably, an infinite number of ways! The particular rules characterize what is computed, but not necessarily how it is computed.

An obvious objection to the idea that rules can specify the results of creativity is that people often "break" the rules in order to produce a more original work of art or scientific idea. Another objection is that, although the criteria of a genre or paradigm might be captured by a set of rules, individuals have their own unique and idiosyncratic styles of thinking within such frameworks. Both objections are instructive, but not decisive. If a creative process breaks the rules, then it must depend either on an arbitrary choice regardless of the rules — as when a musician chooses to play an entirely "random" sequence of notes — or the choice must be governed by further criteria. In either case, however, the performance can be characterized by rules — either rules that allow a random choice or rules for further criteria, assuming that they are computable. Likewise, if an individual has a unique style within a genre, then this style must depend on idiosyncratic criteria governing the creative process. These, too, can be described by rules, assuming that they are computable. If the criteria can be shown *not* to be computable, then Church's thesis would finally have been refuted.

The morals for psychology are clear. Computational power has to do with a working memory for the intermediate results of computations. If creativity is a computable process, then the *output* of the process can be characterized by a set of rules, provided that they are sufficiently powerful.

Neo-Darwinian and Genetic Algorithms

Creative processes take existing elements and combine or modify them in some way. This process, I have argued, is non-deterministic, and it produces something that meets certain existing criteria but is novel for the creator. A direct consequence of this characterization of creativity is that there are only three general classes of algorithm (i.e., computational procedure) on which it could depend.

The first class of algorithms have a neo-Darwinian structure. There are two stages: a generative stage in which ideas are formed in an entirely arbitrary way followed by an evaluative stage, during which the ideas are evaluated according to criteria. Whatever survives, which may be little or nothing, is the result of the process.

The original proponent of this method was the medieval philosopher Ramon Lull. He devised a secret weapon in the war against the infidel: a machine for inventing new ideas. It seems to have consisted in a series of concentric circles on whose edges various words were written (see Gardner, 1982). The user could rotate the wheels into a new position, and then read off the resulting conjunction of ideas aligned over the set of circles. I have often supposed that psychological jargon has a similar genesis. Words such as *cognitive, behavioral,* and *reactive,* are written on one circle; words such as *conflict, dissonance,* and *inhibition,* are written on another. The wheels are spun and out pops, say, *cognitive dissonance* or *reactive inhibition.* The same satirical vein runs all the way from the academy of Lagado in *Gulliver's Travels,* where academics use a similar device to generate new ideas, to the machines for writing pornography in George Orwell's novel, *Nineteen Eighty Four.*

Neo-Darwinism has been advocated by a number of theorists, such as Skinner (1953), Campbell (1960), and Bateson (1979), as the only possible mechanism for creativity. An individual produces a variety of responses, and the contingencies of reinforcement, or some other criteria, select those that are viable and extinguish the remainder. It is crucial to distinguish between a single operation of a neo-Darwinian procedure and its repeated operation, as a familiar example from Dawkins (1976) shows.

A group of monkeys type at random. In theory, one of them could type, by chance, the complete works of Shakespeare. It is a nice theory, but in practice out of the question. Indeed, a long time will elapse before any monkey types even one acceptable English sentence. Even with a universe stuffed full of monkeys, typing away at the speed of light, none of them is the least bit likely to produce Shakespeare's works prior to the final big bang. Random typing seldom meets the constraints of acceptable English, and the number of samples required in order to find one that corresponds to some target text grows exponentially with the number of letters in the target. The problem is the same as the quest for a computer that examines all possible chess games to ensure that it chooses the best possible moves: the number of possibilities increases exponentially with the number of moves ahead that the machine attempts to inspect. The random production of a text is computationally *intractable:* in theory it could succeed, but in practice it works only for small values of the critical variable — such as the number of letters in the target (see Hopcroft & Ullman, 1979).

The problem with the typing monkeys is that nothing *evolves.* They make random choices and that's that. Random methods rapidly cease to be productive if they apply only to a static set of basic concepts. The evolution of species is much more efficient because it does not depend on a single random step. The complete genetic specification of a human being was not assembled from a single shuffling of an unorganized set of genes — an evolutionary step that is no more likely than that a monkey types the works of Shakespeare. In evolution, the existing elements characterize viable species. The process occurs in a large series of recombinations of the successful results of recombinations. New species derive from existing species that have passed a fitness test. Evolution is the archetypal recursive process: it applies to its own successful results.

The recursive aspect of evolution is simulated by the *genetic algorithm* developed by Holland and his colleagues (Booker, Goldberg, & Holland, 1990; Holland, 1975; Holland, Holyoak, Nisbett, & Thagard, 1986). This procedure depends on three main components. The first represents knowledge using a parallel set of conditional rules (a production system) that can classify incoming stimuli and make inferences about them. What is unusual is that the conditional rules are formulated as strings made up from only three basic symbols: 1, 0, and #. These symbols encode by their position in the string the presence of a property (signified by 1), such as large, its absence (signified by 0), or a "don't care" condition (signified by #). A string of these symbols can, accordingly, encode any Boolean combination of properties, including the following sort of rule:

If there is a small, moving, non-striped object, centered in the visual field
    and not adjacent, then move rapidly toward the object.

Two alternative values in the same position are like alleles of the same gene, and the rule as a whole is like a chromosome. The positions in the strings correspond to the basic concepts of the system, the subconcepts in terms of the theory described in chapter 2, so the conditional rules are more complex principles constructed out of the concepts. Because the rules can be used in parallel, they do not need to be logically consistent with one another. Indeed, the competition among them yields a hierarchy of defaults: A specific rule dealing with an exception (e.g., penguins don't fly) will be triggered for relevant cases, but otherwise a more general rule (birds fly) applies by default.

The second component is a method for assessing the usefulness of each rule in solving problems. This component assigns credit to the appropriate rules. If you win a game of chess, then it is easy to assign credit to the move that mated your opponent, but which of the many strategic principles that you followed early in the game should also be credited? The decisions early in the game have no immediate payoff. The program solves this classic puzzle in the following way. Each rule in the production system has a "strength," which affects its chances of being selected for use. If it is used, then its strength is reduced by sharing a proportion of it among the rules that triggered it. Rules that directly attain goals receive a payoff, and the sharing principle ensures that they reward the rules that triggered them, and so on, like a bucket brigade passing the bucket backward from one person to another. Hence, rules early in the sequence will ultimately be rewarded if they tend to occur in successful sequences.

The third component is the genetic program proper, which has a more radical effect on rules. At any one time, some rules will be relatively strong and others relatively weak. The program takes pairs of currently strong rules as "parents" from which it constructs a pair of new rules, which then replace two currently weak rules. The operations used to construct the new rules are analogous to actual genetic mechanisms. The major operator is, thus, a "crossover," in which a randomly selected segment of symbols is exchanged between the pair of strong rules. One can treat each rule as instantiating a more general schema, and Holland et al. (1988) have shown how to make a statistical estimate of the strength of schemas. The rules that are to act as parents can then be chosen on the basis of the strength of the schemas that they instantiate. The result is a rapid increase in the fitness of the population of rules as a whole.

Genetic programs have been successfully applied to many optimization problems in physics, engineering, and games, from the design of more compact VLSI (Very Large Scale Integrated) chips to the acquisition of successful tactics in playing poker. One of their obvious limitations is that their only method of conceptual combination is Boolean. What they cannot construct are relations, such as *is connected to, is identical to,* or *is larger than.* Another limitation is that they are driven by their environment, which provides the feedback that assigns strength to rules. It is not clear, for example, whether a genetic algorithm could be taught to create a work of art or a scientific theory. It would need to internalize the criteria of a genre or paradigm, and such information is not as readily transmitted as is success in a hand of poker or in finding a more optimal design.

Neo-Lamarckian Algorithms

The mechanism for constructing new ideas could be entirely random, and the results could be filtered through a set of constraints. In addition, the whole process could be repeated recursively in multiple stages as in a genetic program. The mechanism is inefficient, but it is the only one available if the generative process cannot itself be guided by criteria, a condition that is the basis of the modern evolutionary synthesis of genetics and natural selection (see Mayr, 1982, p. 537). Yet, if criteria are used in the evaluative stage of the creation of ideas, why not use them instead to constrain the generative stage directly? Why not, indeed, for, unlike species, new ideas could evolve in this way.

Knowledge can guide the generation of new ideas. The great advantage of such a system is its efficiency: if the only ideas that are ever produced are within an existing set of criteria, then the system can save time by avoiding hopelessly implausible conjectures. The most efficient procedure would use all available criteria to guide the generation of new ideas. It would be feasible only for those domains for which an individual has mastered a set of criteria that suffice to guarantee the viability of the results. Because the criteria directly govern the generative stage, it will yield a relatively small number of products, all of which meet the desired characteristics. Hence, the mechanism will be highly efficient. If all available criteria are used to generate an idea, by definition nothing is left for its evaluation. Because creation is not deterministic, there will be certain points where the criteria allow more than one possibility, and so the only way to choose amongst them will be non-deterministic (e.g., by making an arbitrary decision). The process can then occur in just two stages with no need for recursion: first, the generation of ideas according to criteria, and second, an arbitrary selection, where necessary, from among them. I have nicknamed such algorithms neo-Lamarckian because criteria, which may have been acquired by experience, directly govern the generative stage, by analogy with Lamarck's theory of evolution (see Mayr, 1982, p. 354).

Multistage Algorithms

Most forms of creation appear to be neither neo-Darwinian nor neo-Lamarckian. Ideas are generated under the guidance of some criteria, but their initial form leaves something to be desired; that is, the individual applies further criteria to their evaluation and decides that more work needs to be done, and so the ideas are revised, recombined, and so on. The procedure resembles the genetic algorithm in that it is recursive—it is applied repeatedly to its own output—but it differs in that criteria are used in both the generative and evaluative phases of the program.

Many creative individuals do, indeed, work extensively over the results of their earlier efforts, revising and revising and revising. They are clearly using a multistage procedure, but why? Because they are applying criteria at each stage, why don't they apply all of these criteria straightaway in the very first generative stage? Why the need for a time-consuming division of labor over several stages? From a computational standpoint, it would be more efficient to apply all the criteria in the generative stage in a neo-Lamarckian way. It is odd to waste time formulating an inadequate product if you have the ability to perceive its inadequacy and to set matters right.

The fundamental paradox of creativity, as Perkins (1981, p. 128) has remarked, is that people are better critics than creators: their knowledge is more readily available for judgment than for generation. Criticism depends on criteria, as does the generation of ideas, so why is there this difference? The paradox is resolved by a hypothesis about mental architecture. The mind depends on a hierarchy of processors that compute in parallel and that communicate data one to another, but that are not privy to each other's internal operations and representations. These processors also communicate emotional signals that have no internal propositional structure (Oatley & Johnson-Laird, 1987). The case for this "modular" architecture has been made, in various forms, elsewhere (e.g., Fodor, 1983; Johnson-Laird, 1983, chap. 16; & Minsky, 1985). It leads to the isolation of mental representations and procedures so that they may be used by one ability but not others. As an example, consider the ability to whistle a melody. For a computer, the task of perceiving a melody in order to "whistle" it calls for the construction of an internal representation of the intervals in the melody. This same representation could be used to control a program that writes the melody in musical notation. For people, however, the two tasks are entirely different. Most people can whistle a melody; few are able to write it down. The problem is not ignorance of musical notation. Most people who can read music are unable to write down a melody they can whistle. They lack a conscious grasp of the intervals from one pitch to another that occur in the melody. Only after extensive training in musical dictation are they finally able to write down melodies. The difficulty of the task arises because the internal representations that underlie whistling are not available to conscious judgment.

Likewise, some criteria are available to critical processes but not to generative processes. Some of the criteria used in criticism can be communicated verbally, discussed, refined, and debated, but their conscious availability is far from enabling them to control the generation of ideas. At the core of creativity are unconscious procedures composed from the subconcepts described in the previous chapter. When you learn to create, you have to master these unconscious roots of creativity. You have to assemble a set of subconceptual procedures. Conscious verbal instruction alone is useless. The process is similar to the compilation of high-level functions into low-level machine instructions, but human beings have no simple program for this process. It takes work. In mastering new scientific concepts, there is no substitute for working with the concepts. In artistic creativity, there is no substitute for a period of apprenticeship. You learn by imitating successful creators, and by trying to create for yourself in a particular domain. You must enter an almost interminable circle of trying, assessing your failure, and trying once again. Only in this way can you build up the set of subconcepts and principles that govern the generative process: only in this way can you "internalize" the criteria of genre or paradigm. It follows that you cannot learn any general recipe for enhancing your creativity across all domains. Those nostrums and exercises that purport to increase creative ability have no effect on internalizing the criteria of a particular domain: no robust evidence exists to bear out their alleged efficacy. You learn to create by creating, but you must make your attempts in the particular artistic genre or scientific paradigm in which you wish to excel.

We can now resolve the paradox. Because evaluative criteria are readily communicated verbally, whereas generative abilities are unconscious and acquired only laboriously, our critical judgments tend to be in advance of our imaginative abilities. We are, therefore, better critics than creators.

The Three Sorts of Algorithm Are Exhaustive

Given the earlier working definition of *creativity,* the three sorts of algorithm are exhaustive. Suppose, for the sake of argument, that there is a stage of arbitrary combinations; then, apart from the degenerate case of a genre where any possible combination is viable, many products will not be acceptable. Hence, it is necessary to introduce an evaluative stage in which criteria are used to filter out unsatisfactory products. It is necessary to use these two stages recursively in order to arrive at a viable result. This design is neo-Darwinian. Suppose, instead, that there is a single generative stage in which all the criteria are used in creating combinations. In this case, because creation has to be treated as non-deterministic, there will be many possible combinations. Hence, it will be necessary to introduce a selective stage to ensure that at any given time only a single product is created. Because all the criteria have been used in the generative stage, this second stage must depend on arbitrary selection, and there is no need to use the two stages recursively. This design is neo-Lamarckian. If the criteria are divided between generation and selection, then the result is obviously a multistage algorithm. It follows that any creative computation falls into one of the three categories of algorithm.

ARTISTIC CREATIVITY

When a theory leads to a taxonomy, it is instructive to test the theory by trying to apply the taxonomy to relevant domains. The majority of psychological theories of creativity are too vague to determine what sort of computational procedure they would employ (see, e.g., Freud, 1908; Koestler, 1964; Mednick, 1962; Wallas, 1926), but recent theories have been modeled computationally. In the following section I consider some that concern artistic creativity; further on, I take up computational accounts of scientific creativity.

Telling Stories

There is a long tradition of analyzing stories. One of its pioneers, the Russian theorist Vladimir Propp (1928/1958) proposed that folk tales revolve around a small class of actors and actions: a setting in time and space, a hero, the hero's family, the villain, and so on. The Structuralist anthropologist Claude Lévi-Strauss has similarly argued that Greek myths are all instantiations of a single underlying system, which he analyzed in terms of a number of binary contrasts (Lévi-Strauss, 1958/1968). Recently, psycholinguists have proposed rules that purport to analyze the structure of stories. The trouble with all of these proposals, however, is the ease with which theorists can convince themselves that their analyses match the data. Just as numerologists find significant patterns hidden in the Bible, so analysts find the patterns they expect in texts. A simple test will demonstrate whether they are fooling themselves: turn the theory around and try to use it to create stories!

Imagine, as an analogy, that a linguist has proposed a grammar of a language. We can assess its adequacy in two ways. One way is to use the grammar in a parsing test. We check that it assigns plausible analyses to a large sample of grammatical sentences but rejects ungrammatical sentences. The parsing test can be carried out informally in much the same way that theorists analyze myths and stories, but a better procedure is to implement the grammar in a computer program, and to use it to parse a sample of sentences and nonsentences. If the grammar fails to cope with the sample, then something is wrong with it. The fact that it passes the parsing test, however, may merely reflect a lack of imagination in the choice of the sample. As a second test, we can use the grammar to *generate* sentences. Once again, the best procedure is to implement the grammar in a computer program that produces sentences. Because more than one rule can usually be used at any point in the generation of a sentence, the program simulates non-determinism by making an arbitrary decision among the alternatives. A typical output from such a program is as follows:

> The field buys a tiny rain. The rain hops. It burns the noisy sky in the throbbing belt. It buries some yellow wind in it.

Sentences generated in this way may be grammatical, but they are often nonsensical. It is all too easy to devise programs that generate surrealistic prose. Nevertheless, if the grammar is wrong, it will generate ungrammatical sentences, too.

Like any general conjecture, a grammar may err in two ways: it may make errors of omission and so be unable to generate or parse all grammatical sentences, or it may make errors of commission and so generate or parse ungrammatical sentences. Errors of omission are best detected by the parsing test; errors of commission are best detected by the generative test. The generative test is also the decisive one for theories of stories. The traditional structuralist theories fail it irremediably. Lévi-Strauss's theory of Greek myths takes far too much for granted, so that it is impossible even to begin to generate stories using it. The same dismal moral applies to the psycholinguists' story grammars, but here we can pinpoint the problem precisely. Story grammars contain such rules as:

Event → State + Action

This particular rule signifies that an event is composed of a state of affairs followed by an action, but how is one to recognize that a particular sentence (or sequence of sentences) describes a state? Story grammarians have no difficulty in exercising their intuitions when a story is put in front of them, but it is a very different matter to ask them to make these intuitions sufficiently explicit to be used for generating stories.

Some machines for telling stories have been devised; here are two examples of what they do. The first is a fragment from a typical story generated by an early program (Klein, 1975):

> The day was Monday. The pleasant weather was sunny. Lady Buxley was in a park. James ran into Lady Buxley. James talked with Lady Buxley. Lady Buxley flirted with James. James invited Lady Buxley. James liked Lady Buxley. Lady Buxley liked James. Lady Buxley was with James in a hotel. James caressed Lady Buxley with passion. James was Lady Buxley's lover. Marion following them saw the affair. Marion was jealous. . . .

The program develops an embryonic plot that arises from the motives of conflicting personalities. After it has run for long enough to ensure that a state of enmity has arisen between two characters, it contrives for one of them to be killed, and the other to be accused of the murder.

The second example is a story generated by a more recent program (Turner, 1991):

> Once upon a time there was a lady of the court named Maggie. Maggie loved a knight named Grunfeld. Grunfeld loved Maggie. Maggie wanted revenge on a lady of the court named Darlene because she had the berries which she picked in the woods and Maggie wanted to have the berries. Maggie wanted to scare Darlene. Maggie wanted a dragon to move towards Darlene so that Darlene believed it would eat her. Maggie wanted to appear to be a dragon so that a dragon would move towards Darlene. Maggie drank a magic potion. Maggie transformed

into a dragon. The dragon moved towards Darlene. The dragon was near Darlene.

Grunfeld wanted to impress the king. Grunfeld wanted to move towards the woods so that he could fight a dragon. Grunfeld moved towards the woods. Grunfeld was near the woods. Grunfeld fought the dragon. The dragon died. Maggie wanted to live. Maggie tried to drink the magic potion but failed. Grunfeld was filled with grief.

Moral: "Deception serves the devil."

This program, unlike others for telling stories (e.g., Dehn, 1989; Lebowitz, 1985; Meehan, 1976), models the creative part of the process. It is equipped with a set of about 10 existing stories in its long-term memory, and about 30 *heuristics* or rules of thumb for solving a current storytelling goal. These rules have three components: the first transforms a current problem into a slightly different one; the second takes the newly formulated problem and tries to recall a similar one from among the stories in long-term memory; and the third adapts the solution of the recalled problem to fit the current problem. One such heuristic, for example, was given the goal of creating a scene in which a knight accidentally meets a princess. The first component transformed this goal into a modern domain. The recall component found the following story in long-term memory:

John was sitting at home one evening when his dog began acting strange. The dog was scratching at the door and whining for a walk. Finally, John decided to take the dog for a walk. While they were out, John ran across his old friend Pete, whom he hadn't seen in many years. John realized that he would never have run into Pete if his dog hadn't acted so strangely.

Finally, the third component adapted this story to meet the original goal:

One day while out riding, Lancelot's horse went into the woods. Lancelot could not control the horse. The horse took him deeper into the woods. The horse stopped. Lancelot saw Andrea, a Lady of the Court, who was out picking berries.

The heuristic rules include one that allows a constraint to be generalized: for example, the goal that *a knight kills himself* can be generalized to *a knight kills something*. Other heuristic rules look for similar outcomes, switch an intentional action to an unintentional one, or vice versa.

A key idea in the program is that the recall components of the heuristics themselves can call up the creative process recursively. Hence, if a direct attempt to recall an episode of a particular sort fails, then the creative process itself is called, and one of the heuristics modifies the features used in the memory search. If the process now succeeds in recalling an episode, this episode is passed to the original problem and recall succeeds. However, the episode will have been adapted during the recursion (by the third component of the heuristic), and so it will no longer correspond to the episode originally found in memory. Recall itself has become a creative process.

Turner's program leans heavily on the stories that it already has in long-term memory. It transforms them to meet the specific goals set by the user, and so it is a program that solves problems by creating an analogy between its current goal and a problem that has already been solved, that is, a story in its long-term memory. The program is deterministic but it searches for new solutions if it assesses that the current solution is "boring" because it has already been used several times in the past. The algorithm is, accordingly, a species of neo-Lamarckian procedure in which knowledge is used in the immediate generation of a story. Because its performance depends on both the specification of the goal and the existing set of stories in memory, the program simulates only certain aspects of storytelling.

The ability to tell a good story depends on at least three skills. First, a storyteller must be able to imagine an interesting sequence of events. Such a sequence depends on a knowledge of human motives and passions, and of the exigencies of life. The ability to envisage such sequences is, in part, modeled by Turner's program. Second, the storyteller must be able to present the events in a rhetorically effective way, keeping back certain information to heighten suspense, and not necessarily describing what happened in the order in which it happened. Third, the storyteller must describe the events in vivid language that brings to life the characters and their dialogue. Effective stories must work satisfactorily on all three levels, and hence, few stories are completed in a single draft. They depend on a multistage algorithm.

No existing programs are able to tell wholly convincing stories. Without exception, they lack a proper semantic theory. Computers have, at present, only the most rudimentary causal interactions with the world. Hence, their representations of the world are representations only in the eyes of the human users of the program. A program may contain a rule such as:

If X is murdered and Y hates X, then Y may be the murderer of X.

that enables other assertions to be derived, such as:

Marion may be the murderer of Lady Buxley.

but because the program treats such a rule as a string of symbols that generates another string of symbols and has no other notion of meaning, it has no real knowledge of content. Human knowledge is deeper than a merely verbal formulation implies: the *interpretation* of such verbal formulations in terms of models of the world comprises true knowledge, not the merely syntactic manipulations of strings of symbols. Until machines have causal interactions with the world, and the conceptual primitives that enable them to construct models of it, they will have no grasp of meaning, and so they will lack a rich understanding of events. They will be unable to produce new ideas about the world.

The creation of stories, like the creation of scientific theories, depends on a deep understanding of the domain. The attempts to devise storytelling programs have yet to confront this semantic issue. Harold Cohen, who is a successful contemporary painter, has devised a program that draws simple scenes of exotic flora, boulders, and people (see Boden, 1991, for examples of the drawings, and a sketch of the program). He appears to have built into his program both a non-deterministic component ensuring that it never draws the same picture twice, and a rudimentary knowledge of how to form two-dimensional images of three-dimensional objects. Hence, the algorithm appears to be neo-Lamarckian in its architecture.

One of the few domains that avoids the problems of semantics is music. That is, there is no way in which a musical expression, as opposed to a verbal expression, can be judged to be true or false. Music is, thus, an excellent testing ground for theories of creativity, so I examine here three forms of musical creation: the composition of tonal chord sequences, the improvisation of rhythms, and the improvisation of tonal melodies. Readers who know nothing about music may choose to skip the following sections, but I have done my best to make them comprehensible even to nonmusicians. Those who do choose to read on should treat music as an abstract language with no semantics. Of course, music stirs the passions. No one knows why. Nor does anyone know why human beings enjoy being emotionally moved by music or any other form of art.

Tonal Chord Sequences: A Multistage Algorithm

Tonality is the organizing principle for nearly all Western music. It developed over several hundred years of European music, and it continues to serve much 20th-century music, including compositions by Stravinsky and Bartok, and latter-day minimalists, such as Terry Riley and John Adams. It is also the foundation of all popular music, from rock to reggae, and of most modern jazz. The essence of tonality is that a piece of music is at any moment located in a particular key, that is, a subset of notes (a scale) in which one note (the key note or *tonic*) serves a central function, and other notes stand in distinct musical relations to it. The key of C major, for example, is based on the following notes, which can be sung in the familiar ascending scale (do, re, mi, fa, sol, la, ti, do):

```
C    (I)
D    (II)
E    (III)
F    (IV)
G    (V)
A    (VI)
B    (VII)
C    (I)
```

where the Roman numerals denote the seven pitches making up a key, I = tonic, and so on. If the reader sings this scale, the point to notice is that the final "do" sounds very similar to the initial one, though they are in fact an octave apart (i.e., the frequency of the vibrations in the final C in the scale is twice that of the initial one).

Most tonal music consists of a melody accompanied by a sequence of chords. A chord is several notes of different pitches that are sounded together. The notes, C E G, make up the chord of C major, and the notes, G B D, make up the chord of G major. Both chords are of the same type: they consist of a root (I), a note a major third above the root (III), and a note a fifth above the root (V). Any chord based on these intervals is a *major chord*. These two chords differ only in that they are based on different roots, C and G, respectively. The important components of a chord sequence are, accordingly, the sequence of roots of the chords making up the sequence, and the particular intervals that occur in each chord. Tonality is based on a space defined by three principal axes: octaves, major thirds, and fifths (see Krumhansl, 1990; Longuet-Higgins, 1987, sect. II).

Although much has been written about tonal chord sequences, most theories have fallen into the same traps as have psychological theories of creativity. On the one hand, they are vague—too vague, at least, to be modeled in computer programs; on the other hand, they lack sufficient computational power to do the job. Thus, from Rameau (1722/1971) to Forte (1979), theorists have described chord sequences in informal ways equivalent to only a minimum of computational power. When one attempts to make these theories explicit, they translate into finite-state machines of the sort illustrated in simplified form in Fig. 4. (Eigen & Winkler, 1983), where the Roman numerals denote the roots of the chords with respect to the key (i.e., I = the tonic). This machine generates a chord sequence by starting in its initial state, S_0, and making transitions from one state to another by moving along the arrow connecting them. The symbol above

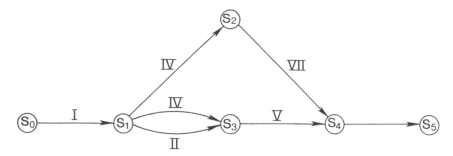

FIG. 4. A finite-state device for generating chord sequences.

each arrow is generated as the machine moves from one state to the next. Thus, the machine might produce the following sequence of symbols:

I   II   V

which denotes a very common chord sequence in tonal music. The types of chord are not shown in the figure, but in classical music they usually consist of those notes that occur in the particular key. Thus, the notes comprise a major chord for I and V, but a minor chord for II, for example, in the key of C, the II chord consists of the root, D, a note a minor third above the root, F, and a note a fifth above the root, A. A major chord on II would have introduced the note of F-sharp, which is foreign to the key.

The machine depicted in Fig. 4 is not deterministic, because there are different choices available in at least one state (S_1). Some modern theorists, inspired by the statistical theory of information, have added probabilities to the different arrows where there are such choices. Their aim is to model the frequencies with which different chords occur (see, e.g., Moles, 1966).

Finite-state machines are far too weak to give a proper account of tonal chord sequences, which need significantly more computational power. Perhaps surprisingly, this claim is easier to confirm for modern jazz than for classical music. Jazz uses about six main types of chord. Here are the three most frequent sorts in the key of C, although they can occur in any key:

C major seventh	(mj7)	C	E	G	B
C dominant seventh	(7)	C	E	G	B♭
C minor seventh	(m7)	C	E♭	G	B♭

where the symbols in parentheses are the typical abbreviations used in jazz notation. The chords may be played with additional notes of various sorts, and in many different voicings and inversions.

A phenomenon unique to jazz enables us to assess the computational power needed to generate chord sequences: the same underlying chord sequence can be performed in many different variations. To capture these variations, Steedman (1982) proposed a set of grammatical rules that generate variations on a given underlying sequence. The rules take as their input a simple underlying sequence, such as the "twelve-bar blues." This sequence entered jazz at its very beginning, but continues to inspire musicians:

I	I	I	I7
IV7	IV7	I	I
V7	IV7	I	I

where "I" denotes a simple major chord on the tonic, and each vertical bar-line separates a measure, which in jazz typically consists of four beats (see the section further on about rhythm, for a description of measures). Steedman's rules produce as one possible variant, a sequence popularized by Charlie Parker:

Imj7		VIIm7	III7	VIm7	II7	Vm7	Vb7
IVmj7		IVm7	VIIb7	IIIm7	VI7	IIIbm7	VIb7
IIm7		VIbm7	IIb7	Imj7	IIIb7	VIbmj7	IIb7

where the final symbol IIb7 stands for a dominant seventh chord with a root on IIb, for example, D♭ in the key of C, which leads back to the tonic at the start of the chord sequence. To a jazz musician, this sequence is an obvious alternative version of the twelve-bar blues, although it may strike the naive listener as quite different. The similarity is nevertheless apparent in structural terms: the first 4 measures move from the tonic (I) to the preparation for the IV chord that occurs in the 5th and 6th measures, the next 4 measures lead back to the tonic (I) in the 11th measure. The underlying sequence maintains the tonic through the 12th measure, whereas Parker's variant introduces a "turn-around" that prepares for the opening bar of the next chorus.

Steedman's rules are equivalent to a context-sensitive grammar. They allow one chord to be substituted for another in certain contexts. Such a grammar corresponds to more computational power than a finite-state machine. If, however, a program generated the underlying sequences rather than taking them for granted as Steedman's grammar does, then perhaps the grammar could be weaker. In order to find out, I developed a program that generates, from scratch, complete tonal sequences of the sort used by jazz musicians. In fact, as I show, this program vindicates Steedman's analysis.

The first stage of the program generates underlying chord sequences, such as the rudimentary twelve-bar blues. It uses a context-free grammar, and, when more than one rule applies, it makes an arbitrary choice from among them. The grammar generates, for example, the following eight measures:

| I | V | I | V | I | V | I | I |

which have the structure:

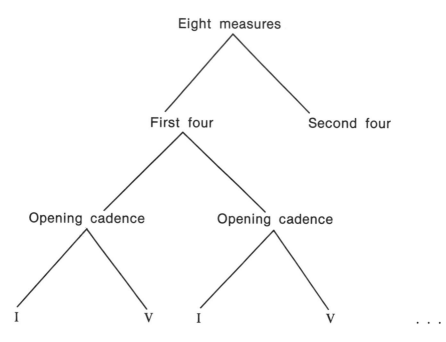

The second stage of the program uses rules to insert chords into the sequence (using the so-called "cycle of fifths"), and to modify existing chords. Hence, given as input the sequence above:

| I | V | I . . .

the rules can transform the penultimate chord into V7 and insert a IIm chord prior to it:

| I | IIm V7 | I . . .

A further application of the rules makes another interpolation:

| I | VIm   IIm   V7 | I   . . .

By progressively working backwards in this way, the final result of this second stage, depending on the particular choices that are arbitrarily made, might be:

| Imj   VIIm   III7 | VIm   IIm   V7 | I   . . .

The third, and final, stage of the program can make other sorts of interpolation, it can substitute one sort of chord for another, and it adds the full symbols denoting the type of chord.

The grammatical rules for making the interpolations in the second and third stages of the program are sensitive to context. They work progressively backward from certain chords that are structurally important, such as a V chord leading to the tonic, I. The only way to calculate which chords to interpolate so as to arrive at a target chord is either to work backward in this way or to use the same computational power to count the number of chords to be interpolated prior to the target. Hence, the rules rely on a memory for the results of intermediate computations—in particular, a memory for each of the results of the previous applications of the rules. The use of context-sensitive rules is essential, as is the use of a working memory for the progressive interpolations, and so the computational power needed to produce the chord sequences does indeed transcend the power of a finite-state machine, such as the one illustrated in Fig. 4. The point of exploiting this greater computational power is to produce chord sequences with a more complex, and presumably more interesting, structure. The end result is more intricate than the output of a finite-state machine.

In practice, the composition of chord sequences depends on a multistage procedure. They are rarely composed, in their finished form, in a single, unrevised series of mental operations; normally, a sequence is refined over several phases of work. The composer tries one idea and then revises it. In jazz, a chord sequence may even evolve over several generations of musicians. I conjecture that whenever a creative process calls for more than minimal computational power, it will depend on a multistage procedure. Such a procedure can exploit a variety of different, and perhaps modular, sources of knowledge. Of course, composers do not need to rely entirely on their working memories in order to carry out complex computations. Notation is a substitute for memory. Other arts similarly make available to the artist a "memory" for intermediate results: the unfinished picture, text, or poem, is itself an intermediate result. Nevertheless, external aids to memory cannot eliminate the need for working memory. The creative process has to occur internally before its results can be recorded externally.

The Improvisation of Melodies:
A Neo-Lamarckian Algorithm

Musical improvisation, like other extempore performances, occurs rapidly and with no opportunity for mistakes to be corrected. It calls for the artist to have internalized sufficient criteria to guarantee that the results are at least acceptable. It also calls for a procedure that runs in "real time": there is no possibility of trying out different possibilities, and then selecting the preferred one. Any extempore form of creation is almost certainly based on a neo-Lamarckian algorithm in which all the criteria are used in generating ideas. If they allow more than one possibility, then an arbitrary choice must be rapidly made from among them. Given the limitations of human processing capacity, the algorithm should use only a minimal amount of working memory. By foregoing any great demands for the storage of intermediate results, the process is maximally efficient. It enables the musician to create music as rapidly as possible, but it is equivalent to the use of a finite-state machine. This lack of computational power can be compensated for by the richness of the chord sequence.

The case that I have considered in some detail is improvisation in modern jazz (see Johnson-Laird, 1991). Like other forms of musical improvisation, it depends on two components: the ability to make up an extempore melody, and a background knowledge of structures that form a foundation for the melodic improvisation. In jazz, these structures are tonal chord sequences that the musicians know by heart. The chord sequences, as we have seen, are not improvised, but composed or borrowed from the compositions of other musicians, such as George Gershwin and Jerome Kern.

As a result of years of improvisatory practise, jazz musicians can navigate their way through chorus after chorus of the chord sequence and create a seemingly endless series of melodies appropriate to its harmonic implications. They are able to produce such melodies, if need be, at the fastest rate that they can physically perform on their instruments: at a rate of about 10 notes per second. Virtuosos such as Charlie Parker seldom, if ever, play wrong notes: each phrase dovetails with the harmonic implications of the chord sequence. Evidently, jazz musicians have an internal representation of the musical criteria governing the generation of melodies. Because a melody consists of two principal components, a rhythm and a sequence of pitches, I consider both of these components. The key assumption in each case is that the mind of the improviser can be modeled by a machine using minimal computational power.

Rhythm

Most music has a metrical pulse in which beats occur at a regular interval of time, and the sequence forms a group of two, three, four, or more beats, which is repeated over and over with an emphasis on the first beat in each group, for example:

    | 1   2   3   4 | 1   2   3   4 | . . .

where the vertical lines indicate the beginning of each new group (the *measure* or *bar*), and the numbers indicate each of the equally spaced beats in the measure. This regular meter provides the framework for rhythm (see, e.g., Lerdahl and Jackendoff, 1983), but meter is not merely the number of beats in the measure: It has a more complex structure. Each beat can also be subdivided in a regular way. Longuet-Higgins and Lee (1984) have shown that such groupings can be captured by a simple context-free grammar, which makes explicit the structure of measures. A good example is the contrast between two beats to the measure that are each subdivided into three, and waltz time of three beats to the measure that are each subdivided into two. One measure in these two meters contains the same number of units (six), but, as the grammar shows, the structures of the two sorts of measure are different. A measure of the first sort has the following structure:

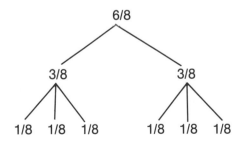

where the label "1/8" is a conventional unit for the duration of a note. Such a tree diagram represents a grouping of events, which can equally well be representing by the following bracketing:

    (((1/8)(1/8)(1/8)) ((1/8)(1/8)(1/8)))

A measure of waltz time, however, has a different grouping of the same six units:

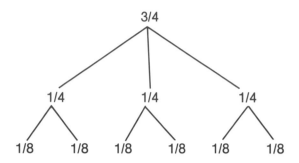

Leonard Bernstein's song, "America" (from *West Side Story*) wittily alternates measures of these two sorts.

A regular subdivision of each beat yields a strong feeling of one meter nested within another. Such simultaneous meters, however, generally occur only at two adjacent levels. The mental principles underlying meter seem able to cope with two or three levels, at most. Likewise, they do not cope easily with two independent meters at the same level. It takes work to internalize the ability to tap simultaneously, say, four beats to the measure with one hand and three beats to the same measure with the other hand. Typically, musicians first learn the overall rhythmic pattern that the two meters make, and then learn how to divide it appropriately between the two hands. West African music, which is polyrhythmic in this way, is also acquired by a similar technique of learning the overall pattern of the simultaneous meters.

The maximum number of beats that can be apprehended as making up an undivided measure is probably 7 ± 2—George Miller's (1956) magical number. Beyond that the meter is subdivided. Even with seven beats to the measure, musicians are likely to divide the measure into a pattern, such as: $3 + 2 + 2$. In realizing the first beat of the measure, musicians have to retain in working memory only a representation of the remaining beats in the measure. It follows that there is no need for a stack of unlimited depth. A limited fixed-capacity working memory will suffice for a proper conception of metrical structure.

Rhythms are created within the framework of a meter, and as many theorists have pointed out (e.g., Povel, 1984), the critical feature of a rhythm is the sequence of onsets of its notes. Hence, if you clap the rhythm of a familiar piece, such as "We all live in a yellow submarine", listeners will be able to identify it. Clapping, of course, provides information only about onset times. The principles for improvising a rhythmic phrase are best described in two stages. Underlying each rhythmic phrase is a prototype, which is common to a whole family of related rhythms. The prototype, in my view, is defined in terms of three categories of events for each beat (Johnson-Laird, in press). The most significant event is a syncopation, which is the occurrence of a relatively long note at an unexpected place – as though it has been displaced and starts in anticipation of its proper place in metrical structure (see Longuet-Higgins & Lee, 1984, for a precise account). The next most significant event is a note on the beat. All other possibilities, including notes that last through the beat and rests (i.e., silences), are of equal but minimal significance. Hence, each of the following instances in waltz time is a member of the same family:

The notation represents notes of the following durations, respectively:

	3/8	1/8		1/8	1/8	
	3/8	1/16	1/16	1/4		
	3/8	1/16	1/16	1/8	1/8	

The family is based on the following prototype of significant events:

The measure consists of a 1/2 note followed by a 1/4 note. This simple prototype can be treated as an underlying representation of a rhythm from which all members of the family are derived. Any variant on the underlying-rhythm is allowed provided that no change occurs to the first important event for each beat. Hence, a rhythm such as:

is not a member of the family we are discussing because it contains a note on the second beat of the measure, which differs from the prototype. A given underlying rhythm can be realized in many different versions, which are the different members of the same family. The particular principles for families of rhythms are specific to genres.

At the highest level of organization, a melody is a sequence of phrases. They can vary in length from less than a measure to several measures, and a good musician aims for variety. An improviser tends to have little conception of what notes to play beyond the current phrase, and even that may contain a surprise. To paraphrase a remark of the novelist E.M. Forster, the improviser's maxim is: How do I know what I am improvising until I hear what I play? Hence, what holds a series of improvised phrases together is not any complex architectural design, but the chord sequence, which is repeated chorus after chorus as the basis for generating ideas. No explicit musical plan appears to govern the structure of an improvisation above the level of individual phrases. There seem to be no strong aesthetic principles at stake, and no strong intuitions about a good organization other than that it should contain variety.

Although the principles for improvising rhythmic phrases are best described in two stages, as I have done, one of the tasks of the musician learning to improvise is to master the principles in a way that minimizes the load on working memory. Both the generation of underlying rhythms and their transduction into actual phrases can be carried out by finite-state machines, and, in fact, the two devices can be collapsed into a single finite-state machine that creates rhythms. The arbitrary choice of one alternative principle over another yields phrases of various lengths.

The most elusive aspect of jazz timing is *swing,* a propulsive and joyous rhythmic feeling that impels all the best performances. "What is swing?," an importunate fan demanded. "If you have to ask," the late Louis Armstrong replied, "you'll never know." Some theorists locate swing in the tendency for jazz musicians to divide each beat into triplets, but this convention is shared by other genres, such as rock-'n'-roll, which seldom attain the swing of a great jazz performance. When one examines the actual durations of notes, it is difficult to discern the underlying principles of swing (cf. Schuller, 1989, Appendix II). No one, so far, has pinned down the phenomenon, at least in an explicit way that can be put into a computer program.

Melody and Pitch

A melody is made up of phrases, which are rhythmic sequences of pitches. Several theories have been proposed about the choice of pitches in an improvised jazz solo. One hypothesis—the null hypothesis, in effect—is that the musician merely chooses any note from among those in the current chord of the chord sequence. This procedure perpetrates errors of both commission and omission: it leaps wildly around from a low note to a high note in a most unmelodic way, and it fails to use *passing notes,* notes that are not in the current chord but that pass from one such note to another in a way that adds to the melodic character of the improvisation. A good guide to the improvisation of a sequence of pitches in jazz is the bass line. The bass player improvises such sequences to fit the chord sequence, but typically in a rhythmically simple way: a steady "walking" bass of four beats to the measure, which maintains the metrical pulse for the benefit of all the musicians. Figure 5 shows a few measures from a typical improvised bass line; and a passing note occurs in the third measure.

A second theory was proposed by Ulrich (1977), who wrote: "Sequences of motifs are woven together to form a melody. Rather than constantly inventing new motifs, the musician modifies old ones to fit new harmonic situations." The same idea underlies a program devised by Levitt (1981), to improvise melodies. Its input is a chord sequence and an existing melody. The program divides up the existing melody into two measure fragments, reassembles them in a different random order, and then modifies the notes, where necessary, so that they fit the chord sequence. The procedure is deterministic — given the same input, it produces the same improvisation but it could be easily modified so as to incorporate an element of non-determinism: a different random reordering could be made for each chorus. This notion of reordering an existing melody, however, is a major departure from human performance. Musicians all use motifs some of the time, but no improviser, apart perhaps from a complete beginner, uses them all of the time. It is much easier in the long run, as any competent performer

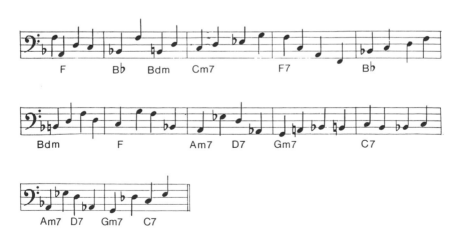

FIG. 5. Some measures from an improvised bass line.

will tell you (see, e.g., Sudnow, 1978), to learn to make up new melodies. The task of committing to memory a vast set of motifs, choosing them at random, and modifying them to fit the current exigencies of the chord sequence, is far too demanding.

A third theory is that improvised melodies depend on principles that specify an aesthetically pleasing contour (Johnson-Laird, 1988a, 1988b). Roughly speaking, a bass player chooses a sequence of notes that are fairly close to one another in pitch, and then, for the sake of variety, introduces one or two larger leaps in pitch, and so on. These principles, I assume, call for only a minimal use of computational power, so their output should be captured by a regular grammar. The contour determines the approximate choice of pitch, and the harmonic constraints of the current chord narrow the choice still further. The constraints as a whole sometimes reduce the choice to a single pitch, but more often there is a small set of possibilities, from which the final choice is made arbitrarily. To test the feasibility of this theory, I have modeled it in two computer programs.

The first program generates a typical walking bass line, given as input a string of symbols denoting a chord sequence—a string of the sort generated by the algorithm for tonal chord sequences. It uses a regular grammar to generate a contour in terms of small or large steps, specifies the harmonically feasible notes within the current step in the contour—both from within the chord and from the set of passing notes—and finally, chooses randomly from the resulting set (unless the constraints narrow the choice down to a single note). Figure 6 shows a fragment from one of its improvisations. Its performance is at the level of a moderately competent beginner. By design, it makes no use of motifs or chromatic runs. By oversight, it has an imperfect grasp of passing notes. Nevertheless, it illustrates the feasibility of the central theoretical claim: in order to improvise, musicians need to use only a limited memory for the results of intermediate computations. The small processing capacity of working memory suffices, and so the underlying mechanism is a finite-state machine. Its performance can be characterized by a regular grammar or by a context-free grammar that contains no recursive rules.

The second program improvises melodies. It uses a regular grammar to generate a rhythmic phrase to fit two measures of a chord sequence, that is, the input to the program is once again a string of chord symbols. The rhythm is then assigned pitches by a contour grammar: the number of notes in the contour must obviously be the same as the number of notes in the rhythm. The machinery of the bass-line algorithm is then used to generate the feasible pitches for a note, and a random choice is made from them.

This theory of improvisation can be summarized as follows. The musicians know by heart the chord sequences of many pieces. These sequences are consciously accessible and readily communicated. Like all tonal se-

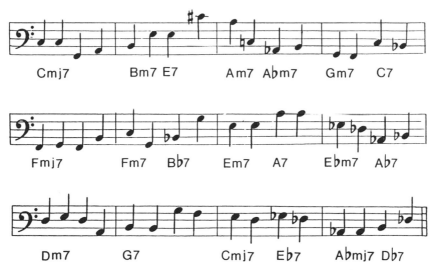

FIG. 6. Some measures from a bass line generated by the computer program.

quences, their composition calls for considerable computational power, although in practice this power is mediated by the use of notation. The musicians also have in their heads a set of profoundly unconscious principles that control the process of melodic improvisation. These principles are acquired at the cost of considerable effort. They are compiled from innate subconceptual primitives, and they embody the principles for generating rhythms and melodic contours. They contain a tacit knowledge of tonal harmony, and they enable the musician, in effect, to determine a "scale" of notes that fits the current chord in the sequence, and from which the notes to be played are chosen. The program for improvising melodies is neo-Lamarckian, and the principles it uses can be modeled by a regular grammar. How these principles are represented in the mind remains entirely unknown. They may, for instance, depend on a form of parallel distributed processing. Unfortunately, it is nearly impossible to obtain evidence that would pinpoint the details of the process.

SCIENTIFIC CREATIVITY

Scientists carry out a variety of activities. They make observations and compute summary statistics, they devise general laws that describe phenomena, they seek theories that explain these laws, and they frame hypotheses based on these theories and design experiments to test them. All these activities call for imagination, although the most notable form of innovation occurs in the development of a new, and perhaps revolutionary, scientific theory. Students of scientific thinking have recently begun to develop computable theories of many of these activities.

The development of quantitative laws, for example, depends on induction, and it has been simulated in the BACON series of programs (Langley, Simon, Bradshaw, & Zytkow, 1987). One of these programs was able to derive Kepler's third law of planetary motion from the appropriate numerical data. Human subjects who discovered the law in an experiment seemed to use the same method of progressively modifying a hypothesis in the light of discrepancies between it and the data. Theoretical assumptions serve as heuristics that constrain BACON's search, and, if these assumptions are strong enough, they enable the program to deduce a law directly from the data. The program DALTON models the use of unobservables in scientific theories. It postulates that molecules are composed of atoms that are conserved in chemical reactions, and so it is able to infer the atomic constituents of substances produced by chemical reactions. The development of an explanatory theory, Simon (in press) claimed, is a similar process. It starts with a representation of the phenomena, and this representation imposes constraints that may allow an explanation to be inferred from the data. Scientists carry out experiments to test laws and theories, and the program KEKADA models the heuristics that they use in planning experiments, including their strategy in response to a surprising observation, that is, determining its scope, and then searching for its underlying mechanism (Kulkarni & Simon, 1988). The program's heuristics enable it to search through the space of possible experiments, guiding its selection of each successive experiment. Still other programs emulate decisions between two competing explanations of the same data (e.g., Shrager & Langley, 1990).

The conception of science underlying these machines appears to be based on three important assumptions:

- Observations yield sets of facts.
- A theoretical explanation is a set of assumptions from which the facts can be deduced.
- A theory can be falsified by empirical observations.

Each one of these views is controversial, and has been opposed by certain philosophers. Quine (1953) has famously argued against the distinction between facts and theoretical assumptions: "Our statements about the external world face the tribunal of sense experience not individually but only as a corporate body." Explanations, according to Harman (1973) and Thagard (1989), need not logically entail the facts that they explain.

Scientific theories cannot be falsified, because of the need to assume that certain auxiliary assumptions hold during the process of testing (Duhem, 1914/1954). My concern, however, is not so much with these methodological matters as with the psychological processes underlying scientific creativity.

The generation of new knowledge often depends on analogy, so I consider, first, attempts to build analogical engines, a topic that we encountered in Turner's (1991) program for storytelling. Next, I examine the creation of innovative scientific concepts and the phenomenon of incommensurability that arises in both science and children's intellectual development. My aim is to distinguish between changes in belief and changes in concepts; to do so, I propose a theory of conceptual revolutions. I illustrate the theory by applying it to a test case: the scientific development of the concept of motion. A major issue is whether the creative and analogical machines accurately model the mental processes of scientists. In my view, they suffer from an inadequate representation of knowledge; I argue, therefore, that mental models are central to scientific creativity.

Analogy as a Source of Novel Ideas

Analogy, it is sometimes said, is the only source of novel ideas. In science, theories have been inspired by analogies between the heart and the pump, the moon and falling objects, the atom and the solar system, and so on (Hesse, 1966). Most theories of the discovery and use of analogies postulate four stages in the process:

1. The search for an identification of a source, that is, a domain that furnishes a potentially useful analogy.
2. The mapping of certain information from the source to the target domain that has triggered the search for an analogy, perhaps because it presents a problem.
3. The use of the new information to reason about the target domain.
4. The evaluation of the success or failure of the analogy.

As an example, consider an experimental study carried out by Gick and Holyoak (1980, 1983). They were interested in the extent to which a helpful analogy would assist their subjects in solving a difficult problem. The problem, originally investigated by Duncker (1945), is to devise a way to use x-rays to cure an internal tumor in a case where rays powerful enough to destroy the tumor will damage the healthy surrounding tissue. Holyoak and Gick gave their subjects a story that contains the kernel of an idea that would solve the x-ray problem. The story recounts how a general besieging a fortress successfully overcame resistance by dividing his army into small groups that attacked the town at different points. An analogous solution to the x-ray problem is to take several sources of weak x-rays and to direct their beams from different locations so that they converge on the tumor. The subjects who heard the story were slightly more likely to solve the x-ray problem, and, if they were explicitly advised to bear the story in mind, then a significantly higher proportion of them solved the problem.

The subjects did not immediately realize that the fortress story was a helpful analogy. Part of their problem may have been that they did not automatically try to map the relations within the source onto the target problem. In other words, the separation of the process into a search stage followed by a transfer of information is slightly artificial: the search is conducted, in part, by seeking domains that can be interrelated by such a transfer of information. Some experimental results suggest that relatively superficial similarities between a target problem and a source may be important in the search (e.g., Gentner & Ratterman, 1987; Ross, 1989). According to Faries and Reiser (1988), however, when subjects are trying to solve programming problems in LISP, they look for analogies that have a structural relation to the task at hand. Their search among problems that they have solved is also more successful if they have had to label them for future reference. Another factor that affects performance is the need for an analogy: unless you run into difficulties, as Holyoak and Thagard (1989) pointed out, you are unlikely to start looking for a helpful analogy.

Several theories have been developed to explain the transfer of information. Gentner (1983, 1989) and her colleagues have argued that there is no fixed semantic agenda for the information that is transferred, and that reasoners tend to transfer higher order relations, such as causation, rather than simpler lower order relations and properties. Thus, what is presumably carried over from the fortress story to the x-ray problem is the notion of splitting a force into separate components that are then applied from different directions.

Holyoak and Thagard (1989) have argued that concepts in the target problem activate a source problem by way of conditional rules. Thus, the rules yield the following sort of links between the two domains:

Source		Target
army	-----------	x-rays
fortress	-----------	tumor
capture	-----------	destroy

They have implemented this theory in a program, but they have to provide the appropriate rules that form such links as:

x-rays → Force → Weapon → Army

These rules, they claim, are likely to be learned by human beings as part of conceptual development. Once the source domain has been activated in this way, the sequence of operations that solved the problem in the source domain is carried over to the target domain, regardless of whether it contains higher order relations or simple properties. Thus, the successful sequence of operations in the fortress problem is: split the force up into smaller units, and apply the separate forces from different directions. Keane (1985, 1988) has similarly argued that the goal structure of the target problem has a direct bearing on the search and mapping processes. These theories, accordingly, offer an account of both the search stage and the transfer stage.

In the search for a useful analogy, there is a vast space of potentially relevant knowledge — so vast that an unconstrained search based on rules that link concepts will take exponentially longer as the number of relevant domains increases. Moreover, the appropriate domain cannot be found by a process of successive approximation. Several potential methods might provide a way out of this difficulty. The search might be based, for example, on a single-step global comparison rather than on a chain of inferences. It may yield only partial analogies, and then call for the structure of the source itself to be modified before the transfer of information. How scientists find useful analogies is, thus, a problem that has yet to be solved. Theories so far have either finessed it or have relied on helpful programmers to cut the search space down to a feasible size. Many intellectual revolutions appear to depend neither on analogies nor changes in beliefs, but on changes in concepts. What constitutes a change in concepts is itself a mystery, let alone how such changes occur, but I propose an answer to both these puzzles in the next section.

The Nature of Conceptual Development

Conceptual knowledge is often incomplete. It is incomplete in some cases because lay individuals are happy to leave matters to experts (Putnam, 1975). Few people know how to determine, for example, whether a substance is gold, an animal is rabid, or a vase is porcelain. Certain concepts, however, are incomplete for everyone, and indeed our knowledge of all natural kinds is incomplete and potentially revisable in the light of further discoveries. Incomplete concepts can still be used as a basis for thought, and conceptual development occurs precisely because certain concepts are incomplete.

Incompleteness suggests that the growth of knowledge is a mere accumulation of information. It may be so in certain domains, but some concepts do turn out to be wrong. They fail to square with how the world works, or they fail to distinguish different entities, or they make false distinctions between entities that are really the same. Science, Oscar Wilde remarked, is the history of dead religions, and among the false gods that scientists have abandoned are earlier concepts of space, motion, light, heat, combustion, life, reproduction, and many, many others. They have all undergone profound revolutions, which were made possible because of the inadequacy of previous conceptions. This inadequacy, in turn, often reflected an incomplete notion that was, at best, only dimly grasped by its proponents.

There is increasing evidence that conceptual revolutions also occur in children's intellectual development (see particularly the work of Susan Carey, e.g., 1985). She pointed out, for example, that preschool children's conception of death differs radically from the adult notion (Carey, 1988). She wrote: "According to the child's understanding, the dead live on, in altered circumstances (under the ground, for example)." She quoted the following conversation with her young daughter, Eliza, to illustrate the point:

Eliza: How do dead people go to the bathroom?
Susan: What?
Eliza: Maybe they have bathrooms under the ground.
Susan: Dead people don't have to go to the bathroom. They don't do anything; they just lie there. They don't eat or drink, so they don't have to go to the bathroom.
Eliza: But they ate or drank before they died—they have to go to the bathroom from just before they died (triumphant at having found a flaw in Carey's argument).

Children, and many adults, seldom articulate explicit theories. They have no access to the subconcepts underlying their everyday concepts. Yet the changes in these concepts, which Carey and her colleagues have observed, do appear to bear out her main thesis. She has argued that the meaning of each concept in a theory depends on its relations to the other concepts in the theory. The claim is reminiscent of the Structuralist thesis that concepts cannot be defined in isolation from one another. It led Carey to make the further claim that ". . . new concepts may arise that are not definable in terms of concepts already held" (Carey, 1991), and to the view that children's concepts may be incommensurable with adult's concepts in a way that parallels the incommensurability of concepts before and after a scientific revolution.

In the analysis of conceptual development, we need to characterize the original concepts and the new concepts, and to determine the nature of the change. We also need to explain the underlying mechanism for such changes, that is, the nature of the process that leads from the earlier concepts to the later ones. Inductive generalization can lead to the addition of new information to a concept—information that fleshes out an incomplete concept — but conceptual revolutions in childhood and science do not depend merely on the accumulation of knowledge. What is striking in current analyses is the lack of computational theories, which are not to be found in either psychological studies of children's development, or philosophical and historical studies of the development of scientific concepts. Those who develop machines for thinking in psychology and artificial intelligence have only just begun to address the issue of conceptual change. To grasp what is at stake in a conceptual revolution, I begin with the striking phenomenon of incommensurability.

The Incommensurability of Concepts

Scientists sometimes have an insight into a problem that leads to a radically new concept. A classic case is Archimedes's insight into the displacement of water by an object. For Simon (In press), these cases are a result of the triggering of a production, which gives access to relevant knowledge. This process may occur when a scientist recognizes that a particular observation conforms to a known principle, but if a new idea depends merely on the triggering of productions, then the relevant knowledge was already implicit in the production system, and, in that case, the discovery is not so novel. Similarly, when a scientist proposes a new theory to replace one that has been falsified, it may transcend existing elements of knowledge. That is why new theories can be so difficult for scientists of the old guard to understand. When Copernicus proposed that the earth moved round the sun, for instance, many people could not understand the theory. For them, the earth by definition was the fixed center of the universe. A revolutionary scientific theory, as Kuhn (1970) has argued, is often incommensurable with the theory it supplants. Those who adhere to the rival theories are often unable to communicate properly: "In a sense that I am unable to explicate further," Kuhn commented, "the proponents of competing paradigms practice their trades in different worlds" (p. 150).

Philosophers sometimes take Kuhn to be arguing that rival theorists cannot communicate with one another at all, that their arguments are mutually incomprehensible, and so the choice between the theories ultimately depends on entirely irrational factors. This interpretation is a profound misconstrual of his remarks (see Kuhn, 1970, p. 199). Incommensurability is not the same as incomprehensibility.

Permanent incomprehensibility arises from the lack of a shared subconcept. Suppose, for example, we remove the successor and zero functions from the primitives of recursive function theory (see chapter 2): we are left with only the list-processing functions. Any inductive algorithm will then be unable to construct arithmetic functions: It could learn to do list-processing, but not addition or multiplication. List-processing *Homo erectus* could never understand the arithmetical concepts of *Homo sapiens,* which would be permanently incomprehensible. *Erectus* could make a shopping list, but not make change. What Alpha Centaurian concepts, you might wonder, would be permanently incomprehensible for us? Any positive answer to this question would, of course, be meaningless for us, but if Church's thesis is correct, then we can take comfort from having mastered what little is needed to construct computable functions and to grasp that certain functions are not computable. Human beings are equipped with a rich set of concepts, and they have the wit to supplement their inadequate working memories with notation. There is every chance that the riddle does not exist: human beings may be able to grasp any concept.

If incomprehensibility arises from the lack of shared primitive concepts, what underlies incommensurability? One factor is language. Kuhn (1970, pp. 201–202) argued that because key words have been learned from their direct application to exemplars, rival theorists cannot provide an account of the relevant criteria for the use of a word in a neutral language. What they have to do is to recognize their plight and to develop the ability to translate their ideas into a shared vocabulary. More is at stake, however, than language. A scientific revolution is a conceptual revolution:

> Think of the sun, moon, Mars, and earth before and after Copernicus; of free fall, pendular, and planetary motion before and after Galileo; or of salts, alloys, and a sulphur-iron filing mix before and after Dalton. Since most objects within even the altered sets continue to be grouped together, the names of the sets are usually preserved. Nevertheless, the transfer of a subset is ordinarily part of a critical change in the network of interrelations among them. Transferring the metals from the set of compounds to the set of elements played an essential role in the emergence of a new theory of combustion, of acidity, and of physical and chemical combination. (Kuhn, 1970, pp. 200–201)

When scientists switch allegiance from an old theory to a new one, they change their conceptual systems, but why isn't such a change merely a change in beliefs? After all, if your concepts change, your beliefs change too, because, as I showed in the previous chapter, concepts and thoughts are mutually interrelated. Thagard (1992) described a hierarchy of degrees of conceptual change. Among the weakest changes is the mere acquisition of a new belief, such as that whales eat sardines. Stronger changes include modifications in the organization of concepts, such as the switch from *metals are compounds* to *metals are elements,* but, once again, why isn't that just a change in belief?

When you change your conceptual system, it feels quite different from changing your beliefs. The point is not only a phenomenological one. If you come across a novel theory relatively late in life, you may change your beliefs.

You may accept, for example, that space-time is curved by the presence of matter, yet you may fail to develop a full grasp of the theory to the point where it can help you to solve problems. You have not properly internalized the theory. Your beliefs have changed, and you pay lip service to them, but they are not backed up by a proper grasp of the underlying concepts.

To develop a new theory is, as Nersessian (in press) has argued, to develop the ability to form novel explanatory models of the world. Of course, you can build novel models out of existing concepts, and in this case the process is straightforward. The problem is, therefore, to make sense of the distinction between a change in concepts and a change in beliefs. No solution exists in the literature, but the distinction can be drawn in terms of the theory of mental models. The crux is the ineffable nature of the subconceptual primitives on which all models ultimately devolve.

A change in beliefs is a recombination of existing concepts. It is equivalent to the composition of a new ad hoc concept (see chapter 2). Both processes depend on concepts that are already in play and that are automatically compiled into their primitive subconcepts. When a conceptual change occurs, however, certain existing concepts cease to be common coinage. The concepts of the new theory are not new combinations of them, but alternatives to them. Those who wish to understand the new theory cannot do so merely on the basis of their current concepts: they have to acquire new concepts, high-level structures based on a new combination of primitive subconcepts. This process is laborious. It is similar, as I remarked earlier, to the compilation of a high-level function into low-level machine instructions. A novel conceptual combination of ineffable subconcepts is not readily communicable. It cannot be immediately acquired from knowledge by description, but only by retracing the steps of the original theorist, a process aided by knowledge from acquaintance with the phenomena. That is why the new theory depends on more than a mere change in beliefs: changes in beliefs are fashioned from existing high-level concepts, changes in concepts depend on going back to basics, back to the set of innate subconcepts.

Concepts in science normally fit together in a seemingly consistent theory. When a conceptual revolution occurs, typically certain concepts — those at the more operational or observational level — remain more or less unchanged, whereas other concepts may undergo a radical change. In terms of the relations among concepts that derive from semantic information, there are five possible relations between an old concept and a new concept, but one of the them is equivalence. Hence, four possible sorts of change to individual concepts are possible:

1. The new concept may be a generalization of the old: it may bring together two hitherto separate conceptions within a single integrative idea.

2. The new concept may be a specialization of the old: it may be formed by splitting the old notion into two or more distinct notions.
3. The new concept may overlap with the old: it retains some components of the old, but the two notions diverge with respect to other subconcepts.
4. The new concept is a radical alternative to the old: it is, in effect, the conceptual analogue of the negation of the old idea.

What complicates the picture is that a new theory may reflect different sorts of changes to the different concepts underlying it. I will illustrate the possibilities by examining a well-known case of conceptual evolution in science.

The Development of the Concepts of Motion and Speed

Aristotle's conception of motion in his *Physics* is, in essence, that motion is change of place. There are two sorts of motion: natural motion, such as the motion of weighty objects toward the center of the universe (the earth); and compulsory motion, which is contrary to nature, such as when one object causes another to move by contact. Aristotle's notion of speed is evident from his discussion of the effects of the density of the medium through which motion occurs (*Physics,* 215b, 1–6) and from the following remarks: "And since every magnitude is divisible into magnitudes . . . it necessarily follows that the quicker of two things traverses a greater magnitude in an equal time, an equal magnitude in less time, and a greater magnitude in less time, in conformity with the definition sometimes given of the quicker" (*Physics,* 232a, 25–29).

Many aspects of Aristotle's theory resemble our everyday conception of motion. The fundamental concept remains change of location over time (see Miller & Johnson-Laird, 1976, sect. 7.1). Objects move, some as a result of their own power, some as a result of the actions of others upon them. Many individuals to this day suppose that an object that has been forced to move has an "impetus" that inevitably peters out bringing the object to rest (McCloskey, 1983). Motion can be perceived, and a grasp of the subconcepts of motion enables individuals to construct a kinematic spatial model:

t   t′

where at one moment, t, an object is at one location and at a later moment, t', it is at another location. A computer program can construct such a representation. Given a verbal input, such as, "The disk moved," it can use a compositional semantics to construct a procedure that, when evaluated, creates such a kinematic model in which the position of the disk changes over time. Conversely, given such a model that was derived from a rudimentary perceptual system, a descriptive procedure could construct, the verbal description, "The disk moved."

Many aspects of the corresponding human system of mental models are outside conscious awareness. How do our models represent space? Presumably, not by the real-number continuum, which is far too dense to be accommodated within a finite organ such as the brain. How do models represent time? They could do so spatially, but, in fact, they do not need to *represent* time: they can directly use real time, that is, the model itself unfolds in time. Hence, although we can construct models of motion, they do not make available to us any foundational theory of space and time. They are based on unconscious subconcepts that enable us to construct models. These models represent motion as change of location over time: They embody that assumption, although we may have no theory of motion that we can make explicit. We can build models of the world based on perception and use our concept of motion to describe what is going on or to evaluate the truth of an assertion. We can also use our concept of motion to envisage what is going on from a verbal description, but if asked what motion is, we may be stumped for an answer, just as individuals are unable to provide any sort of analysis for other quasi-primitives such as ownership. What subjects do when they are asked to define the verb *to move* is to reply with synonymous or similar verbs, such as *travel* or *advance* (see Johnson-Laird, 1983, chap. 10). The concept certainly depends on more basic notions, but we have no immediate conscious access to them. What we have is the machinery of tacit subconcepts that enables us to envisage models.

The revisions in the Aristotelian conception of motion took many centuries to accomplish and are quite diverse. Thus, Newtonian mechanics applies uniformly to both natural and unnatural motions. Aristotle's theory drew an unnecessary distinction, which, as I have mentioned, many people continue to make. Thus, Newton brought together two hitherto separate conceptions within a single integrative idea (a change of type 1 in the classification of the previous section).

Consider the concept of speed. Like Aristotle, we can conceive one object as moving faster than another if at one time they are lined up together and at a later time the first object is ahead of the second. Hence, the grasp of the notion that the disk moves faster than the square enables us to construct this kinematic model:

$$t \qquad\qquad t'$$

In such models of real physical possibilities, the concept of *moves faster* seems entirely coherent. It elicits a kinematic model, which is based on a subconceptual notion of speed. It corresponds quite closely to the conception of motion that young children (and some adults) possess, a correspondence that was noted by Kuhn (1964). We may also, as Kuhn suggested, see that an object is moving very fast if we receive only a blurred impression of it:

$$t \qquad\qquad t'$$

The Aristotelian conception of speed fails to fit the world. What seems like a coherent notion leads to uncertainty and confusion. If, as Kuhn imagined, someone poses to us Galileo's famous thought experiment, then we will probably be uncertain how to answer. Galileo envisaged the following set up:

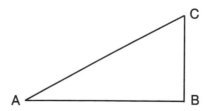

There are two objects: one moves down the inclined plane from C to A, and one moves down the vertical plane from C to B. They move without friction, and when they reach the bottom, they have acquired the same speed. The question is: which object moved faster? Galileo was able to show that the Aristotelian conception of speed can lead one to argue that the two objects move at the same speed, that the object moving down the vertical plane is faster, or that it is slower. What the paradox hinges on is the fact that speed should not be attributed to the motion as a whole, but to its parts.

A similar problem arises in the following dialogue, freely adapted from the late Richard Feynman's lectures on physics (Feynman, Leighton, & Sands, 1963):

Policeman: You were going at 60 miles an hour.

Driver: That's impossible. I was traveling only for seven minutes. How can I go 60 miles an hour when I wasn't going for an hour?

Policeman: What I mean is that if you kept going the same way as you were going, then in the next hour you would go 60 miles.

Driver: The car was slowing down, so if I kept on going that way it would not go 60 miles. And in any case, if I had kept on going, I would have run into the wall at the end of the street!

Policeman: What I mean is if you went one second, you would go 88 feet.

Driver: There is no law against going 88 feet per second.

At this point, the policeman might reply, "Tell that to the judge!", but what he should reply is that 88 feet per second is the same as 60 miles per hour. In other words, the driver's speed *at the moment* the radar beam was reflected back from the car was 60 miles per hour. This concept of instantaneous speed must be distinguished from the Aristotelian conception of average speed. The two notions are implicit in the two sorts of model that embodied our original concept: the model of one object overtaking another (average speed), and the model of the blurred object moving rapidly across the visual field (instantaneous speed). Nowhere in our original conception, however, were the two notions distinguished in any way. The new concept of instantaneous speed requires us to draw that distinction, and ultimately to grasp the idea of dividing distance by time while making the interval of time smaller and smaller, and observing the result as the interval tends toward the infinitely small. This change in concepts is formed by splitting the old notion into two distinct notions (a change of type 2 in the earlier classification).

This change in our conception of motion does not bring us fully up to date. Newton assumed that the mass of a moving object is constant, where mass is the inertia of an object, that is, how hard it is to get the object to move by applying a force to it. In the special theory of relativity, mass is no longer constant, but increases with the velocity of an object. As that velocity approaches the speed of light, the momentum of the object approaches infinity. The new concept overlaps with the old—they have the notion of inertia in common—but the two concepts differ with respect to other subconcepts (a change of type 3 in our classification).

Our models have provided a fixed framework so that we were able earlier to talk of the disk moving faster than the square with respect to that framework. The principle of relativity requires the laws of physics to be the same for both a stationary observer and observers moving with a uniform velocity in a straight line in relation to the fixed observer. Hence, if the observers are in a spaceship, they have no way of detecting whether they are at rest or moving with a uniform velocity unless they can look outside. This change replaces one conception— motion in relation to an absolute frame of reference—by its negation (a change of type 4).

In summary, a revolution in science leads to a new sort of model, which typically embodies concepts that are not observable in the world. As this brief history of the concept of motion shows, the development of a theory may lead to different sorts of changes within the organization of the subconcepts in the theory. What distinguishes these changes from those that underlie changes in beliefs is that they are not merely modifications of an existing organization of high-level concepts. They depend on the construction of new concepts from primitive subconcepts, a process that is comparable to the development of a new genre of art.

The Role of Mental Models in Science

Do the machines that have been developed to simulate scientific thinking use the same sorts of procedures as human thinkers? This question arises most critically with respect to the representation of knowledge (see Johnson-Laird & Legrenzi, In press). Theories based on semantic networks or production systems postulate that scientific thinking consists of the manipulation of language-like expressions, but thinking, as I have argued, is the manipulation of models, not linguistic formulas. Operations on formulas perhaps occur when a mathematician searches for a formal proof within a calculus, but otherwise the basis of thought appears to be our understanding of problems and ideas, and this understanding depends on the construction of mental models. Indeed, many scientific discoveries appear to derive from images or mental models of phenomena. The classic cases include Snell's law of the reflection of light, Kekulé's discovery of the structure of benzene, and, according to Wise (1979), Maxwell's development of the field theory of electromagnetism. As Wise pointed out, models generate problems, and their answers may in turn call for a reorganization of the representations themselves. A model may, thus, be misleading, and a theorist may be forced to transcend the customary conception of events. Galileo's discovery of the law of inertia, for example, called for an idealization of actual movements, which are affected by friction, and for putting to one side the customary representation of falling objects, which seems closer to Aristotle's account of motion.

The intuitions of scientists bear out the claim that thinking is based on models rather than on expressions in a mental language. Of all the quotations on this point, the remarks of Einstein in a letter in Hadamard (1945) are the most apt:

> The words or the language, as they are written or spoken, do not seem to play any role in my mechanism of thought. The psychical entities which seem to serve as elements in thought are certain signs and more or less clear images which can be "voluntarily" reproduced and combined.
>
> There is, of course, a certain connection between those elements and relevant logical concepts. It is also clear that the desire to arrive finally at logically connected concepts is the emotional basis of this rather vague play with the above mentioned elements. But taken from a psychological viewpoint, this combinatory play seems to be the essential feature in productive thought — before there is any connection with logical construction in words or other kinds of signs which can be communicated to others.

The role of imagery in scientific discovery thus seems indubitable (see also A. Miller, 1984; Valéry, 1894/1972), and it calls for procedures that can construct and manipulate models of phenomena rather than quasi-linguistic strings of symbols. The distinction between the two sorts of formats is structural: models have a structure that corresponds to our conception of the world; linguistic representations have a syntactic structure, which can be remote from our conception of the world. For instance, a model represents a quantified expression by a set of tokens corresponding to the set of individuals; a linguistic representation represents such an expression by a syntactically structured formula (as in the predicate calculus).

The machinery for constructing models is largely automatic and unconscious. You have no access to the underlying brain processes — the firing of neurons, events at synapses, and so on — and you have no access to the nuts-and-bolts of concepts — the manipulation of innate subconcepts. Even the nature of your own concepts is something that you have to discover if you wish to make them explicit. The heuristic procedures for manipulating models in ways that yield novel concepts are, for the most part, unknown. Yet, we can be reasonably certain about three aspects of the process.

First, it is unlikely to be based on a neo-Darwinian or genetic algorithm. Conceptual innovation would be all but impossible if thinkers had to try arbitrary possibilities in the way in which Edison discovered a suitable substance for the filaments of electric light bulbs. Likewise, it is not based on a neo-Lamarckian procedure: the constraints of knowledge on the play of ideas are not such as to guarantee success in a single manipulation. Hence, the most likely algorithm is a multistage one.

Second, given a multistage algorithm, the initial models must be based on existing knowledge: you cannot construct a model without some existing concepts. Likewise, the play of ideas in the experimental manipulations of models are likely to be partially constrained by knowledge: the process of exploration is unlikely to be entirely arbitrary. Once again, we see how important knowledge is to the process of creation: there are no general recipes that enhance your creativity over all domains. Furthermore, a common effect of expertise is to close off intellectual horizons. Hence, one needs a delicate balance between the necessary mastery of subconcepts and the freedom to manipulate the resulting models.

Third, the construction of a new model, as a result of repeated mental experimentation and evaluation in relation to the world, may lead to an explanation. Success, if it is achieved, depends on many iterations of the process. It takes further work, however, to derive an explicit theory from such a model. Repeated construction of models can lead to the compilation of new concepts from the set of subconcepts, but the conscious grasp of the nature of these concepts is not immediate. Scientists only gradually discover the full import of their novel ideas (see, e.g., Gruber, 1974, on Darwin's intellectual development).

CONCLUSIONS

Creativity can be modeled by three sorts of machine. The first sort uses a neo-Darwinian process of arbitrary generation followed by critical evaluation. The evolution of species depends on the recursive use of such a procedure. Despite many claims to the contrary, it is an open question whether ideas ever evolve in this way. The second sort of machine uses a neo-Lamarckian process in which the criteria of a genre are used to generate ideas, and an arbitrary choice is made whenever they generate more than one possibility. This process appears to be unique to those arts and practices of daily life that depend on extempore performance. It makes possible the rapid creation of satisfactory results. The third sort of machine uses a multistage algorithm in which some criteria are used to generate ideas and others are used to evaluate them. This procedure is used in many kinds of artistic and scientific creation.

Profound creativity, as in the the invention of a new artistic genre or a new scientific paradigm, is poorly understood. It is a rare phenomenon, but it appears to depend on a multistage procedure that leads ultimately to a novel model. Universal constraints on the process are unlikely to exist, and so, it is hard to resist concluding that the problem is computationally intractable. Any algorithm needs to be guided by some sort of constraints — not too many and not too few — and these constraints arise from knowledge of the particular domain, but their specific nature only becomes apparent to us after the fact. When we learn how scientists have fashioned a new paradigm, we discover something of the knowledge lying behind their innovation. It invariably seems remarkable that they had the right knowledge and skills at the right time, because so much could have been relevant a priori.

Epilogue

A complete theory of thinking should enable us to construct thinking machines, that is, devices that instantiate the theory and that are able to deduce, induce, and create. Any account that fails this test is, at best, a sketch for a cognitive science. Past theories had neither this goal before them nor the conceptual equipment needed to achieve it. Nowadays, as I have shown in this book, computable theories of thinking are under construction. The most comprehensive designs are for machines that can make deductions. Surprisingly, creative machines seem easier to develop than inductive machines. The reason is that a machine that generates, say, poetry by using a simple neo-Darwinian algorithm does not need any profound theory of meaning: creativity is in the mind of the beholder, and so readers bring to a poem all of their interpretative skills. A successful inductive program, however, needs a semantic theory of its own.

Existing machines, as I have argued, have no adequate grasp of meaning. Meaning calls for primitive subconcepts that *relate* internal models to the external world, and such relations call for machines to have richer causal interactions with the world. They need to perceive; they need to act. Lacking these abilities, computer representations based on semantic networks, production systems, or other quasi-linguistic formats, have not begun to grapple with the necessary semantics. It follows that machines for the creation of ideas are still more remote. The agenda for future studies of innovation, particularly in science, should be headed with this item: develop a proper theory of meaning and representation. That theory, as I have hinted more than once, is likely to invoke models with structures that correspond to our conceptions of the world.

Finally, is there something demeaning about the mechanization of thought? Surely, the skeptic is likely to protest, humanity should not be dragged down to the level of machines? Doesn't the very idea destroy the possibility of moral, aesthetic, and spiritual values? I think not. The error is in a demeaning conception of machines. Leonardo da Vinci, one of the founders of Renaissance humanism, observed the human body with the eye of a mechanical engineer. His goal was to delineate the machine. The poet, Paul Valéry, who, as I mentioned earlier, sought to understand the sources of creativity, spoke of the writer as an engineer and of poetry as a machine made from language. In an essay on the method of Leonardo (Valéry, 1894/1972), he wrote, ". . . every combination of elements made to be perceived and judged depends on a few general laws and on a particular adaptation, defined in advance for a foreseen category of minds to which the whole is specially addressed; and the work of art becomes a machine designed to arouse and assemble the individual formations of those minds". To examine the mind with the eye of a cognitive scientist is a culmination of three great traditions: the humanistic, the biological, and the computational. Its goal is to delineate the mind as a machine.

References

Allen, R.B. (1988). Sequential connectionist networks for answering simple questions about a microworld. *Proceedings of the Tenth International Conference of the Cognitive Science Society* (pp. 489–495). Hillsdale, NJ: Lawrence Erlbaum Associates.

Anderson, J.R. (1983). *The architecture of cognition.* Hillsdale, NJ: Lawrence Erlbaum Associates.

Angluin, D. (1978). Inductive inference of formal languages from positive data. *Information and Control, 45,* 117–135.

Armstrong, S.L., Gleitman, L.R., & Gleitman, H. (1983). What some concepts might not be. *Cognition, 13,* 263–308.

Bara, B.G., Carassa, A.G., & Geminiani, G.C. (1984). Inference processes in everyday reasoning. In D. Plander (Ed.), *Artificial intelligence and information-control systems of robots.* Amsterdam: Elsevier.

Bar-Hillel, Y., & Carnap, R. (1964). An outline of a theory of semantic information. In Y. Bar-Hillel (Ed.), *Language and information.* Reading, MA: Addison-Wesley.

Barsalou, L.W. (1987). The instability of graded structure: implications for the nature of concepts. In U. Neisser (Ed.), *Concepts and conceptual development: Ecological and intellectual factors in categorization.* Cambridge, England: Cambridge University Press.

Bateson, G. (1979). *On mind and nature.* London: Wildwood House.

Berwick, R.C. (1986). Learning from positive-only examples: The subset principle and three case studies. In R.S. Michalski, J.G. Carbonell, & T.M. Mitchell (Eds.), *Machine learning: An artificial intelligence approach, Vol. II.* Los Altos, CA: Morgan Kaufmann.

Beth, E.W. (1971). *Aspects of modern logic.* Dordrecht, Holland: Reidel.

Bledsoe, W.W. (1977). Non-resolution theorem proving. *Artificial Intelligence, 9,* 1–35.

Bledsoe, W.W., Boyer, R., & Heaneman, W. (1972). Computer proofs of limit theorems. *Artificial Intelligence, 3,* 27–60.

Boden, M. (1991). *The creative mind: Myths and mechanisms.* New York: Basic Books.

Booker, L.B., Goldberg, D.E., & Holland, J.H. (1990). Classifier systems and genetic algorithms. In J.G. Carbonell, (Ed.), *Machine learning: Paradigms and methods.* Cambridge, MA: MIT Press.

Boolos, G., & Jeffrey, R. (1989). *Computability and logic.* (3rd ed.). Cambridge, England: Cambridge University Press.

Braine, M.D.S. (1978). On the relation between the natural logic of reasoning and standard logic. *Psychological Review, 85,* 1–21.

Braine, M.D.S., Reiser, B.J., & Rumain, B. (1984). Some empirical justification for a theory of natural propositional logic. *The Psychology of Learning and Motivation, Vol. 18.* New York: Academic Press.

Bruner, J.S., Goodnow, J.J., & Austin, G.A. (1956). *A study of thinking.* New York: Wiley.

Byrne, R.M.J., & Johnson-Laird, P.N. (1989) Spatial reasoning. *Journal of Memory and Language, 28,* 564–575.

Campbell, D.T. (1960). Blind variation and selective retention in creative thought as in other knowledge processes. *Psychological Review, 67,* 380–400.

Carey, S. (1985). *Conceptual change in childhood.* Cambridge, MA: MIT Press.

Carey, S. (1988). Conceptual differences between children and adults. *Mind & Language, 3,* 167–181.

Carey, S. (1991). Knowledge acquisition: Enrichment or conceptual change? In S. Carey, & R. Gelman, (Eds.), *The epigenesis of mind: Essays on biology and cognition.* Hillsdale, NJ: Lawrence Erlbaum Associates.

Cheng, P.W., & Holyoak, K.J. (1985). Pragmatic reasoning schemas. *Cognitive Psychology, 17,* 391–416.

Cheng, P.W., & Novick, L.R. (1991). Causes versus enabling conditions. *Cognition, 40,* 83–120.

Clark, H.H. (1969). Linguistic processes in deductive reasoning. *Psychological Review, 76,* 387–404.

Clocksin, W.F., & Mellish, C.S. (1981). *Programming in Prolog.* Berlin: Springer-Verlag.

Collins, A.M., & Quillian, M.R. (1969). Retrieval time from semantic memory. *Journal of Verbal Learning and Verbal Behavior, 8,* 240–247.

Cook, S.A. (1971). The complexity of theorem proving procedures. *Proceedings of the Third Annual ACM Symposium on the Theory of Computing,* 151–158.

Craik, K. (1943). *The nature of explanation.* Cambridge, England: Cambridge University Press.

Crick, F. (1988). *What mad pursuit.* New York: Basic Books.

Dawkins, R. (1976). *The selfish gene.* Oxford: Oxford University Press.

Dehn, N. (1989). *Computer story-writing: The role of reconstructive and dynamic memory* (Tech. Rep. 792). New Haven: Yale University, Department of Computer Science.

DeJong, G.F., & Mooney, R. (1986). Explanation-based learning: An alternative view. *Machine Learning, 1,* 145–176.

DeSoto, L.B., London, M., & Handel, L.S. (1965). Social reasoning and spatial paralogic. *Journal of Personality and Social Psychology, 2,* 513–521.

Dickstein, L.S. (1978). The effects of figure on syllogistic reasoning. *Memory & Cognition, 6,* 76–83.

Dietterich, T.G., & Michalski, R.S. (1983). A comparative review of selected methods for learning from examples. In R.S. Michalski, J.G. Carbonell, & T.M. Mitchell (Eds.), *Machine learning: An artificial intelligence approach.* Los Altos, CA: Morgan Kaufmann.

Dowty, D.R., Wall, R.E., & Peters, S. (1981). *Introduction to Montague semantics.* Dordrecht, Holland: Reidel.

Duhem, P. (1954). *The aim and structure of physical theory* (P. Wiener, Trans). Princeton: Princeton University Press. (Original work published 1914)

Duncker, K. (1945). On problem solving. *Psychological Monographs, 58* (Whole No. 270).

Edelman, G.M. (1987). *Neural Darwinism: The theory of neuronal group selection.* New York: Basic Books.

Ehrlich, K., & Johnson-Laird, P.N. (1982). Spatial descriptions and referential continuity. *Journal of Verbal Learning and Verbal Behavior, 21,* 296–306.

Eigen, M., & Winkler, R. (1983). *Laws of the game: How the principles of nature govern chance.* Harmondsworth, Middlesex: Penguin.

Erickson, J.R. (1974). A set analysis theory of behavior in formal syllogistic reasoning tasks. In R. Solso (Ed.), *Loyola Symposium on Cognition, Vol. 2.* Hillsdale, NJ: Lawrence Erlbaum Associates.

Estes, W.K. (1986). Array models for category learning. *Cognitive Psychology, 18,* 500–549.

Evans, J.St. B.T., Barston, J.L., & Pollard, P. (1983). On the conflict between logic and belief in syllogistic reasoning. *Memory & Cognition, 11,* 295–306.

Faries, J.M., & Reiser, B.J. (1988). Access and use of previous solutions in a problem solving situation. *Proceedings of the Tenth Annual Conference of the Cognitive Science Society* (pp. 433–439) Hillsdale, NJ: Lawrence Erlbaum Associates.

Feynman, R. P., Leighton, R.B., & Sands, M. (1963). *The Feynman lectures on physics: Vol. 1. Mainly mechanics, radiation, and heat.* Reading, MA: Addison-Wesley.

Fisher, S.C. (1916). The process of generalizing abstraction, and its product, the general concept. *Psychological Monographs,* 21(2, Whole No. 90).

Fodor, J.A. (1975). *The language of thought.* Hassocks, Sussex: Harvester Press.

Fodor, J.A. (1980). Fixation of belief and concept acquisition. In M. Piattelli-Palmarini (Ed.), *Language and learning: The debate between Jean Piaget and Noam Chomsky.* Cambridge, MA: Harvard University Press.

Fodor, J.A. (1983). *The modularity of mind: An essay on faculty psychology.* Cambridge, MA: Bradford Books, MIT Press.

Fodor, J.D., Fodor, J A , & Garrett, M.F. (1975). The psychological unreality of semantic representations. *Linguistic Inquiry, 4,* 515–531.

Forte, A. (1979). *Tonal harmony in concept and practice.* (3rd ed.). New York: Holt, Rinehart & Winston.

Frege, G. (1967). *Begriffsschrift, a formula language, modeled upon that of arithmetic, for pure thought.* In J. Van Heijenoort (Ed.), *From Frege to Gödel: A source book in mathematical logic, 1879–1931.* Cambridge, MA: Harvard University Press. (Original work published 1879)

Freud, S. (1959). Creative writers and day-dreaming. In J. Strachey (Ed. and Trans.), *The standard edition of the complete psychological works of Sigmund Freud, Vol. 9.* London: Hogarth Press. (Original work published 1908)

Gardner, M. (1982). *Logic machines and diagrams* (2nd ed.). Chicago: University of Chicago Press.

Gennari, J.H., Langley, P., & Fisher, D. (1990). Models of incremental concept formation. In J.G. Carbonell (Ed.), *Machine learning: Paradigms and methods.* Cambridge, MA: MIT Press.

Gentner, D. (1983). Structure mapping: A theoretical framework for analogy. *Cognitive Science, 7,* 155–170.

Gentner, D. (1989). The mechanisms of analogical learning. In S. Vosniadou, & A. Ortony (Eds.), *Similarity and analogical reasoning.* New York: Cambridge University Press.

Gentner, D., & Ratterman, M.J. (1987). Analogy and similarity: Determinants of accessibility and inferential soundness. *Proceedings of the Ninth Cognitive Science Society* (pp. 23–35). Hillsdale, NJ: Lawrence Erlbaum Associates.

Gibson, J.J. (1966). *The senses considered as perceptual systems.* Boston: Houghton Mifflin.

Gick, M., & Holyoak, K. (1980). Analogical problem solving. *Cognitive Psychology, 12,* 306–355.

Gick, M., & Holyoak, K. (1983). Schema induction and analogical transfer. *Cognitive Psychology, 15,* 1–38.

Girotto, V., Legrenzi, P., & Rizzo, A. (1991). Event controllability in counterfactual thinking. *Acta Psychologica, 78,* 111–133.

Gödel, K. (1967). On formally undecidable propositions of *Principia Mathematica* and related systems I. In J. Van Heijenoort (Ed.), *From Frege to Gödel: A source book in mathematical logic, 1879–1931.* Cambridge, MA: Harvard University Press. (Original work published 1931)

Gold, E.M. (1967). Language identification in the limit. *Information and Control, 16,* 447–474.

Greene, S. B. (in press). Multiple explanations for multiply-quantified syllogisms: Are multiple models necessary? *Psychological Review.*

Griggs, R.A. & Cox, J.R. (1982). The elusive thematic-materials effect in Wason's selection task. *British Journal of Psychology, 73,* 407–420.

Gruber, H.E. (1974). *Darwin on man: A psychological study of scientific creativity.* London: Wildwood House.

Hadamard, J. (1945). *The psychology of invention in the mathematical field.* Princeton: Princeton University Press.

Hagert, G. (1984). Modeling mental models: Experiments in cognitive modeling of spatial reasoning. In T. O'Shea (Ed.), *Advances in artificial intelligence.* Amsterdam: North-Holland.

Hanson, S.J., & Bauer, M. (1989). Conceptual clustering, categorization, and polymorphy. *Machine Learning, 3,* 343–372.

Hanson, S.J., & Kegl, J. (1987). PARSNIP: A connectionist network that learns natural language grammar from exposure to natural language sentences. *Proceedings of the Ninth Annual Conference of the Cognitive Science Society* (pp. 106–119). Hillsdale, NJ: Lawrence Erlbaum Associates.

Harman, G. (1973). *Thought.* Princeton, NJ: Princeton University Press.

Harman, G. (1986). *Change in view: Principles of reasoning.* Cambridge, MA: Bradford Books, MIT Press.

Hayes-Roth, F., & McDermott, J. (1978). An interference matching technique for inducing abstractions. *Communications of the Association for Computing Machinery, 21,* 410–411.

Heider, F. (1958). *The psychology of interpersonal relations.* New York: Wiley.

Henle, M. (1962). The relation between logic and thinking. *Psychological Review, 69,* 366–378.

Hesse, M. (1966). *Models and analogies in science.* Notre Dame, IN: Notre Dame University Press.

Hewitt, C. (1972). *Description and theoretical analysis of PLANNER* (Report MIT-AI-258). Cambridge, MA: MIT.

Hinton, G.E. (1986). Learning distributed representations of concepts. In *Proceedings of the Eighth Annual Conference of the Cognitive Science Society.* Hillsdale, NJ: Lawrence Erlbaum Associates.

Hobbes, T. (1968). *Leviathan.* Harmondsworth, Middlesex: Penguin. (Original work published 1651)

Hofstadter, D.R. (1982). Can inspiration be mechanized? *Scientific American, 247*(9), 18–31.

Hogarth, R. (Ed.). (1982). *New directions for methodology of social and behavioral science: No. 11. Question framing and response consistency.* San Francisco: Jossey-Bass.

Holland, J.H. (1975). *Adaptation in natural and artificial systems.* Ann Arbor, MI: University of Michigan Press.

Holland, J.H., Holyoak, K.J., Nisbett, R.E., & Thagard, P. (1986). *Induction: Processes of inference, learning, and discovery.* Cambridge, MA: MIT Press.

Holyoak, K.J., & Thagard, P. (1989). Analogical mapping by constraint satisfaction. *Cognitive Science, 13,* 295–355.

Hopcroft, J.E., & Ullman, J.D. (1979). *Formal languages and their relation to automata.* Reading, MA: Addison-Wesley.

Hull, C.L. (1920). Quantitative aspects of the evolution of concepts. *Psychological Monographs, 28* (Whole No. 123).

Hunt, E.B., Marin, J., & Stone, P.T. (1966). *Experiments in induction.* New York: Academic Press.

Hunter, I.M.L. (1957). The solving of three-term series problems. *British Journal of Psychology, 48,* 286–298.

Husserl, E. (1929). Phenomenology. *Encyclopedia Britannica,* 14th ed.

Huttenlocher, J. (1968). Constructing spatial images: A strategy in reasoning. *Psychological Review, 75,* 286–298.

Inder, R. (1987). *Computer simulation of syllogism solving using restricted mental models.* Unpublished doctoral dissertation, Edinburgh University, Edinburgh.

Inhelder, B., & Piaget, J. (1958). *The growth of logical thinking from childhood to adolescence.* London: Routledge & Kegan Paul.

Inhelder, B., & Piaget, J. (1964). *The early growth of logic in the child.* New York: Norton.

Jackendoff, R. (1989). What is a concept, that a person may grasp it? *Mind & Language, 4,* 68–102.

Johnson-Laird, P.N. (1975). Models of deduction. In R.J. Falmagne (Ed.), *Reasoning: Representation and process in children and adults.* Hillsdale, NJ: Lawrence Erlbaum Associates.

Johnson-Laird, P.N. (1983). *Mental models.* Cambridge, MA: Harvard University Press.

Johnson-Laird, P.N. (1988a). *The computer and the mind.* Cambridge, MA: Harvard University Press.

Johnson-Laird, P.N. (1988b). Freedom and constraint in creativity. In R.J. Sternberg (Ed.), *The nature of creativity.* Cambridge, England: Cambridge University Press.

Johnson-Laird, P.N. (1990). *Propositional reasoning: An algorithm for deriving parsimonious conclusions.* Unpublished manuscript, Princeton University, Princeton.

Johnson-Laird, P.N. (1991). Jazz improvisation. In P. Howell, R. West, & I. Cross (Eds.), *Representing musical structure.* London: Academic Press.

Johnson-Laird, P.N. (in press). Rhythm and meter: A theory at the computational level. *Psychomusicology.*

Johnson-Laird, P.N., & Bara, B. (1984). Syllogistic inference. *Cognition, 16,* 1–61.

Johnson-Laird, P.N., & Byrne, R.M.J. (1989). *Only* reasoning. *Journal of Memory and Language, 28,* 313–330.

Johnson-Laird, P.N., & Byrne, R.M.J. (1991). *Deduction.* Hillsdale, NJ: Lawrence Erlbaum Associates.

Johnson-Laird, P.N., Byrne, R. M. J., & Schaeken, W. (1992). Propositional reasoning by model. *Psychological Review.*

Johnson-Laird, P.N., Byrne, R. M.J., & Tabossi, P. (1989). Reasoning by model: The case of multiple quantification. *Psychological Review, 96,* 658–673.

Johnson-Laird, P.N., & Legrenzi, P. (in press). Comments on Simon's theory of science as heuristic search. *Journal of Epistemological and Social Studies on Science and Technology.*

Johnson-Laird, P.N., Legrenzi, P., & Legrenzi, M.S. (1972). Reasoning and a sense of reality. *British Journal of Psychology, 63,* 395–400.

Johnson-Laird, P.N., Oakhill, J.V., & Bull, D. (1986). Children's syllogistic reasoning. *Quarterly Journal of Experimental Psychology, 38A,* 35–58.

Johnson-Laird, P.N., & Steedman, M. (1978). The psychology of syllogisms. *Cognitive Psychology, 10,* 64–99.

Joliecoeur, P., Gluck, M., & Kosslyn, S.M. (1984). Pictures and names: Making the connection. *Cognitive Psychology, 16,* 243–275.

Kahneman, D., & Miller, D. (1986). Norm theory: Comparing reality to its alternatives. *Psychological Review, 93,* 136–153.

Kahneman, D., & Tversky, A. (1972). Subjective probability: A judgement of representativeness. *Cognitive Psychology, 3,* 430–454.

Karmiloff-Smith, A., & Inhelder, B. (1974/1975) 'If you want to get ahead, get a theory.' *Cognition, 3,* 195–212.

Katz, J.J., & Fodor, J.A. (1963). The structure of a semantic theory. *Language, 39,* 170–210.

Keane, M.T. (1985). On drawing analogies when solving problems: A theory and test of solution generation in an analogical problem solving task. *British Journal of Psychology, 76,* 449–458.

Keane, M.T. (1988). *Analogical problem solving.* West Sussex: Ellis Horwood.

Keil, F.C. (1991). The emergence of theoretical beliefs as constraints on concepts. In S. Carey, & R. Gelman (Eds.), *The epigenesis of mind: Essays on biology and cognition.* Hillsdale, NJ: Lawrence Erlbaum Associates.

Kemler Nelson, D.G. (1984). The effect of intention on what concepts are acquired. *Journal of Verbal Learning and Verbal Behavior, 23,* 734–759.

Kintsch, W. (1974). *The representation of meaning in memory.* Hillsdale, NJ: Lawrence Erlbaum Associates.

Klayman, J., & Ha, Y-W. (1987). Confirmation, disconfirmation and information in hypothesis testing. *Psychological Review, 94,* 211–228.

Klein, S. (1975). Meta-compiling text grammars as a model for human behavior. In R.C. Schank, & B. Nash-Webber (Eds.), *Theoretical issues in natural language processing.* Proceedings of Workshop of the Association of Computational Linguistics.

Koestler, A. (1964). *The act of creation.* London: Hutchinson.

Krumhansl, C. (1990). *Cognitive foundations of musical pitch.* Oxford: Oxford University Press.

Kuhn, T. S. (1964). A function for thought experiments. In *Mélanges Alexandre Koyné: II, L'aventure de l'esprit.* Paris: Hermann. (Rep. in Johnson-Laird, P.N. & Wason, P.C. (Eds.), *Thinking.* Cambridge, England: Cambridge University Press, 1976.)

Kuhn, T. (1970). *The structure of scientific revolutions* (2nd ed.). Chicago, IL: University of Chicago Press.

Kulkarni, D., & Simon, H.A. (1988). The process of scientific discovery: the strategy of experimentation. *Cognitive Science, 12,* 139–175.

Kunda, Z. (1990). The case for motivated reasoning. *Psychological Bulletin, 108,* 480–498.

La Mettrie, J.O. de (1912). *Man a machine.* La Salle, IL: Open Court. (Original work published 1748)

Langley, P., Simon, H.A., Bradshaw, G.L., & Zytkow, J.M. (1987). *Scientific discovery.* Cambridge, MA: MIT Press.

Lebowitz, M. (1985). Story telling and generalization. *Proceedings of the Twelfth Annual Conference of the Cognitive Science Society* (pp. 100–109). Hillsdale, NJ: Lawrence Erlbaum Associates.

Lerdahl, F., & Jackendoff, R. (1983). *A generative theory of tonal music.* Cambridge, MA: MIT Press.

Levesque, H.J. (1986). Making believers out of computers. *Artificial Intelligence, 30,* 81–108.

Lévi-Strauss, C. (1968). *Structural anthropology.* London: Allen Lane. (Original work published 1958)

Levitt, D.A. (1981). *A melody description system for jazz improvisation.* Unpublished master's thesis, MIT, Cambridge, MA.

Lewis, C. (1986). A model of mental model construction. *Proceedings of CHI '86 Conference on Human Factors in Computer Systems.* New York: Association for Computing Machinery.

Lindsay, R., Buchanan, B.G., Feigenbaum, E.A., & Lederberg, J. (1980). *Applications of artificial intelligence for chemical inference: The DENDRAL project.* New York: McGraw-Hill.

Longuet-Higgins, H.C. (1987). *Mental processes: Studies in cognitive science.* Cambridge, MA: Bradford Books, MIT Press.

Longuet-Higgins, H.C., & Lee, C.S. (1984). The rhythmic interpretation of monophonic music. *Music Perception, 1,* 424–441.

Mani, K., & Johnson-Laird, P.N. (1982). The mental representation of spatial descriptions. *Memory & Cognition, 10,* 181–187.

Manktelow, K. I., & Over, D. E. (1987). Reasoning and rationality. *Mind & Language, 2,* 199–219.

Markman, E.M., & Seibert, J. (1976). Classes and collections: Internal organization and resulting holistic properties. *Cognitive Psychology, 8,* 561–577.

Markovits, H., & Nantel, G. (1989). The belief-bias effect in the production and evaluation of logical conclusions. *Memory & Cognition, 17,* 11–17.

Marr, D. (1982). *Vision: A computational investigation into the human representation and processing of visual information.* San Francisco: W.H. Freeman.

Mayr, E. (1982). *The growth of biological thought: Diversity, evolution, and inheritance.* Cambridge, MA: Belknap, Harvard University Press.

McCloskey, M. (1983). Naive theories of motion. In D. Gentner, & A.L. Stevens (Eds.), *Mental models,* Hillsdale, NJ: Lawrence Erlbaum Associates.

McCluskey, E.J. (1956). Minimization of Boolean functions. *Bell Systems Technical Journal, 35,* 1417–1444.

McDermott, D. (1987). A critique of pure reason. *Computational Intelligence, 3,* 151–160.

Mednick, S.A. (1962). The associative basis of the creative process. *Psychological Review, 69,* 220–232.

Medvedev, Z.A. (1990) *The legacy of Chernobyl.* New York: Norton.

Meehan, J.R. (1976). *The metanovel: Writing stories by computer* (Tech. Rep. No. 74). New Haven: Yale University, Department of Computer Science.

Michalski, R.S. (1973). Discovering classification rules using variable-valued logic system VL1. *Proceedings of the Third International Joint Conference on Artificial Intelligence, IJCAI* (pp. 162–172). Los Altos, CA: Morgan Kaufmann.

Michalski, R.S. (1983). A theory and methodology of inductive learning. In R.S. Michalski, J.G. Carbonell, & T.M. Mitchell (Eds.), *Machine learning: An artificial intelligence approach.* Los Altos, CA: Morgan Kaufmann.

Mill, J.S. (1950). *A system of logic ratiocinative and inductive.* Toronto: University of Toronto Press. (Original work published 1843)

Miller, A. (1984). *Imagery in scientific thought: Creating 20th-century physics.* Boston, MA: Birkhauser.

Miller, G.A. (1956). The magical number seven plus or minus two. *Psychological Review, 63,* 81–97.

Miller, G.A., Galanter, E., & Pribram, K. (1960). *Plans and the structure of behavior.* New York: Holt, Rinehart & Winston.

Miller, G.A., & Johnson-Laird, P.N. (1976). *Language and perception.* Cambridge, MA: Harvard University Press.

Minsky, M. (1975). Frame-system theory. In R.C. Schank, & B.L. Webber (Eds.), *Theoretical issues in natural language processing.* In P.N. Johnson-Laird, & P.C. Wason (Eds.), *Thinking: Readings in cognitive science.* Cambridge, England: Cambridge University Press.

Minsky, M. (1985). *The society of mind.* New York: Simon & Schuster.

Mitchell, T.M. (1977). Version spaces: A candidate elimination approach to rule learning. *Fifth International Joint Conference on Artificial Intelligence* (pp. 305–310). Cambridge, MA.

Mitchell, T.M., Keller, R., & Kedar-Cabelli, S. (1986). Explanation-based generalization: A unifying view. *Machine Learning, 1,* 47–80.

Moles, A.A. (1966). *Information theory and aesthetic perception.* Urbana, IL: University of Illinois Press.

Montague, R. (1974). *Formal philosophy: Selected papers.* New Haven: Yale University Press.

Mueller, E.T. (1990). *Daydreaming in humans and machines: A computer model of the stream of thought.* Norwood, NJ: Ablex.

Nersessian, N.J. (in press). How do scientists think? Capturing the dynamics of conceptual change in science. In R. Giere (Ed.), *Cognitive models of science: Minnesota studies in the philosophy of science, Vol. 15.* Minneapolis, MN: University of Minnesota Press.

Newell, A. (1990). *Unified theories of cognition.* Cambridge. MA: Harvard University Press.

Newell, A., Shaw, J.C., & Simon, H.A. (1963). Empirical explorations with the Logic Theory Machine. In E. Feigenbaum, & J. Feldman (Eds.), *Computers and thought.* New York: McGraw-Hill.

Newell, A., & Simon, H.A. (1972). *Human problem solving.* Englewood Cliffs, NJ: Prentice-Hall.

Nisbett, R.E., Krantz, D.H., Jepson, D., & Kunda, Z. (1983). The use of statistical heuristics in everyday inductive reasoning. *Psychological Review, 90,* 339–363.

Nisbett, R.E., & Ross, L. (1980). *Human inference: Strategies and shortcomings of social judgement.* Englewood Cliffs, NJ: Prentice-Hall.

Novak, G.S. (1977). Representations of knowledge in a program for solving physics problems. *Proceedings of the Fifth International Joint Conference on Artificial Intelligence, 286–291.*

Oakhill, J.V., Garnham, A., & Vonk, W. (1989). The on-line construction of discourse models. *Language & Cognition, 4,* 263–286.

Oakhill, J.V., & Johnson-Laird, P.N. (1985a). The effects of belief on the spontaneous production of syllogistic conclusions. *Quarterly Journal of Experimental Psychology, 37A,* 553–569.

Oakhill, J.V., & Johnson-Laird, P.N. (1985b). Rationality, memory and the search for counterexamples. *Cognition, 20,* 79–94.

Oakhill, J.V., Johnson-Laird, P.N., & Garnham, A. (1989). Believability and syllogistic reasoning. *Cognition, 31,* 117–140.

Oatley, K., & Johnson-Laird, P.N. (1987). Towards a cognitive theory of emotion. *Cognition & Emotion, 1,* 29–50.

Ohlsson, S. (1984). Induced strategy shifts in spatial reasoning. *Acta Psychologica, 57,* 46–67.

Osherson, D.N. (1974-1976). *Logical abilities in children* (Vols. 1–4). Hillsdale, NJ: Lawrence Erlbaum Associates.

Osherson, D.N., Smith, E.E., & Shafir, E. (1986). Some origins of belief. *Cognition, 24,* 197–224.

Pearl, J. (1986). Fusion, propagation, and structuring in belief networks. *Artificial Intelligence, 29,* 241–288.

Peirce, C.S. (1958). *Selected writings: Values in a universe of chance.* New York: Doubleday.

Pelletier, F.J. (1986). Seventy-five problems for testing automatic theorem provers. *Journal of Automated Reasoning, 2,* 191–216.

Penrose, R. (1989). *The emperor's new mind: Concerning computers, minds, and the laws of physics.* Oxford: Oxford University Press.

Perkins, D.N. (1981). *The mind's best work.* Cambridge, MA: Harvard University Press.

Piaget, J., & Inhelder, B. (1969). *The psychology of the child.* New York: Basic Books.

Poincaré, H. (1929). *The foundations of science: Science and hypothesis, the value of science, science and method.* New York: The Science Press.

Polk, T.A., & Newell, A. (1988). Modeling human syllogistic reasoning in Soar. In *Proceedings of the Tenth Annual Conference of the Cognitive Science Society* (pp. 181–187). Hillsdale, NJ: Lawrence Erlbaum Associates.

Pollock, J. (1989). *How to build a person: A prolegomenon.* Cambridge, MA: Bradford Books.

Polya, G. (1957). *How to solve it* (2nd ed.). New York: Doubleday.

Popper, K.R. (1972). *Objective knowledge.* Oxford: Clarendon.

Povel, D-J. (1984). A theoretical framework for rhythm perception. *Psychological Research, 45,* 315–337.

Power, R.J.D., & Longuet-Higgins, H.C. (1978). Learning to count: A computational model of language acquisition. *Proceedings of the Royal Society (London) B, 200,* 391–417.

Propp, V.I. (1958). *Morphology of the folk tale.* Austin, TX: University of Texas. (Original work published 1928)

Putnam, H. (1975). The meaning of 'meaning.' In K. Gunderson (Ed.), *Language, mind and knowledge: Minnesota Studies in the Philosophy of Science,* Vol. 7. Minneapolis: University of Minnesota Press.

Quillian, M.R. (1968). Semantic memory. In M. Minsky (Ed.), *Semantic information processing.* Cambridge, MA: MIT Press.

Quine, W.V.O. (1953). *From a logical point of view.* Cambridge, MA: Harvard University Press.

Quine, W.V.O. (1955). A way to simplify truth functions. *American Mathematical Monthly, 62,* 627–631.

Quine, W.V.O. (1960). *Word and object.* Cambridge, MA: MIT Press.

Quinlan, R. (1983). Learning efficient classification procedures and their application to chess end games. In R.S. Michalski, J.G. Carbonell, & T.M. Mitchell (Eds.), *Machine learning: An artificial intelligence approach.* Los Altos, CA: Morgan Kaufmann.

Quinlan, R. (1990, September). *Comparing connectionist and symbolic learning methods.* Paper delivered at the Workshop on Computational Learning Theory and Natural Learning Systems, Princeton University.

Rameau J.P. (1971). *Treatise on harmony.* New York: Dover Books. (Original work published 1722)

Reber, A.S. (1985). *The Penguin dictionary of psychology.* Harmondsworth, Middlesex: Penguin.

Reiter, R. (1973). A semantically guided deductive system for automatic theorem-proving. *Proceedings of the Third International Joint Conference on Artificial Intelligence,* 41–46.

Reiter, R. (1980). A logic for default reasoning. *Artificial Intelligence, 13,* 81–132.

Revlin, R., & Leirer, O. Von. (1978). The effects of personal biases on syllogistic reasoning. In R. Revlin & R.E. Mayer (Eds.), *Human reasoning.* New York: Wiley.

Richardson, J.T.E. (1987). The role of mental imagery in models of transitive inference. *British Journal of Psychology, 78,* 189–203.

Rips, L.J. (1983). Cognitive processes in propositional reasoning. *Psychological Review, 90,* 38–71.

Rips, L.J. (1990). Reasoning. *Annual Review of Psychology, 41,* 321–353.

Rips, L.J., Shoben, E.J., & Smith, E.E. (1973). Semantic distance and the verification of semantic relations. *Journal of Verbal Learning and Verbal Behavior, 12,* 1–20.

Robinson, J. A. (1979). *Logic: Form and function.* Edinburgh: Edinburgh University Press.

Rosch, E. (1973). Natural categories. *Cognitive Psychology, 4,* 328–350.

Rosch, E. (1977). Classification of real-world objects: Origins and representations in cognition. In P.N. Johnson-Laird & P.C. Wason (Eds.), *Thinking: Readings in cognitive science.* Cambridge: Cambridge University Press.

Ross, B.H. (1989). Distinguishing types of superficial similarities: Different effects on the access and use of earlier problems. *Journal of Experimental Psychology: Learning, Memory, and Cognition, 15,* 456–468.

Schank, R.C. (1975). *Conceptual information processing.* Amsterdam: North-Holland.

Schank, R.C. (1986). *Explanation patterns: Understanding mechanically and creatively.* Hillsdale, NJ: Lawrence Erlbaum Associates.

Schuller, G. (1989). *The swing era: The Development of Jazz, 1930–1945.* Oxford: Oxford University Press.

Selfridge, M. (1986). A computer model of child language learning. *Artificial Intelligence, 29,* 171–216.

Shrager, J., & Langley, P., Eds. (1990). *Computational models of scientific discovery and theory formation.* San Mateo, CA: Morgan Kaufmann.

Siklossy, L., Rich, A., & Marimov, V. (1973). Breadth first search: Some surprising results. *Artificial Intelligence, 4,* 1–23.

Simon, H.A. (1982). *Models of bounded rationality* (Vols. 1–2). Cambridge, MA: MIT Press.

Simon, H.A. (in press). Scientific thinking. *Journal of Epistemological and Social Studies on Science and Technology.*

Simonton, D.K. (1984). *Genius, creativity, and leadership: Historiometric inquiries.* Cambridge, MA: Harvard University Press.

Singer, J.L. (1978). Experimental studies of daydreaming and the stream of consciousness. In K.S. Pope & J.L. Singer (Eds.), *The stream of consciousness.* New York: Plenum.

Skinner, B.F. (1953). *Science and human behavior.* New York: Macmillan.

Smith, E.E. (1988). Concepts and thought. In R.J. Sternberg & E.E. Smith (Eds.), *The psychology of human thought.* Cambridge: Cambridge University Press.

Smoke, K.L. (1932). An objective study of concept formation. *Psychological Monographs, 42* (Whole No. 191).

Smoke, K.L. (1933). Negative instances in concept learning. *Journal of Experimental Psychology, 16,* 583–588.

Spelke, E.S. (1991). Physical knowledge in infancy: Reflections on Piaget's theory. In S. Carey & R. Gelman (Eds.), *The epigenesis of mind: Essays on biology and cognition.* Hillsdale, NJ: Lawrence Erlbaum Associates.

Sperber, D., & Wilson, D. (1986). *Relevance: Communication and cognition.* Oxford: Basil Blackwell.

Steedman, M.J. (1982). A generative grammar for jazz chord sequences. *Music Perception, 2,* 52–77.

Sudnow, D. (1978). *Ways of the hand.* London: Routledge & Kegan Paul.

Tarski, A. (1956). The concept of truth in formalized languages. In A. Tarski (Ed.), *Logic, semantics, metamathematics: Papers from 1923 to 1938.* Oxford: Oxford University Press. (Original work published 1936)

Thagard, P. (1989). Explanatory coherence. *Behavioral and Brain Sciences, 12,* 435–467.

Thagard, P. (1992). *Conceptual revolutions.* Princeton: Princeton University Press.

Thagard, P., & Holyoak, K.J. (1985). Discovering the wave theory of sound. *Proceedings of the Ninth International Joint Conference on Artificial Intelligence.* Los Altos, CA: Morgan Kaufmann.

Turing, A.M. (1950). Computing machinery and intelligence. *Mind, 59,* 433–460.

Turner, S. (1991). *MINSTREL: A model of storytelling and creativity* (Tech. Note UCLA-AI-N-91). Los Angeles: University of California, Computer Science Department, Artificial Intelligence Laboratory.

Tversky, A., & Kahneman, D. (1973). Availability: A heuristic for judging frequency and probability. *Cognitive Psychology, 4,* 207–232.

Tversky, A., & Kahneman, D. (1982). The simulation heuristic. In D. Kahneman, P. Slovic & A. Tversky (Eds.), *Judgement under uncertainty: Heuristics and biases.* Cambridge, England: Cambridge University Press.

Ulrich, J.W. (1977). The analysis and synthesis of jazz by computer. *Proceedings of the Fifth International Joint Conference on Artificial Intelligence* (pp. 865–872). Los Altos, CA: Morgan Kaufmann.

Valéry, P. (1972). Introduction to the method of Leonardo da Vinci. In *Leonardo Poe Mallarmé: The Collected Works of Paul Valéry* Vol. 8. Princeton: Princeton University Press. (Original work published 1894)

Vygotsky, L.S. (1962). *Thought and language.* Cambridge, MA: MIT Press. (Original work published 1934)

Wallas, G. (1926). *The art of thought.* London: Jonathan Cape.

Wason, P.C. (1960). On the failure to eliminate hypotheses in a conceptual task. *Quarterly Journal of Experimental Psychology, 12,* 129–140.

Wason, P.C. (1966). Reasoning. In B.M. Foss (Ed.), *New horizons in psychology.* Harmondsworth, Middlesex: Penguin.

Wason, P.C. (1977). 'On the failure to eliminate hypotheses . . .' – A second look. In P.N. Johnson-Laird, & P.C. Wason (Eds.), *Thinking: Readings in cognitive science.* Cambridge, England: Cambridge University Press.

Wason, P.C. (1983). Realism and rationality in the selection task. In J.St.B.T. Evans (Ed.), *Thinking and reasoning: Psychological approaches.* London: Routledge & Kegan Paul.

Wason, P.C., & Green, D.W. (1984). Reasoning and mental representation. *Quarterly Journal of Experimental Psychology, 36A,* 597–610.

Wason, P.C., & Johnson-Laird, P.N. (1972). *Psychology of reasoning: Structure and content.* Cambridge, MA: Harvard University Press.

Wason, P.C., & Shapiro, D. (1971). Natural and contrived experience in a reasoning problem. *Quarterly Journal of Experimental Psychology, 23,* 63–71.

Weisberg, R. (1986). *Creativity: Genius and other myths.* New York: W.H. Freeman.

Wetherick, N.E., & Gilhooly, K.J. (1990). Syllogistic reasoning: effects of premise order. In K.J. Gilhooly, M.T.G. Keane, R.H. Logie, & G. Erdos (Eds.), *Lines of thinking: Reflections on the psychology of thought: Vol. 1. Representation, reasoning, analogy and decision making.* Chichester: Wiley.

Whitehead, A., & Russell, B.A.W. (1910). *Principia mathematica* (Vol I). Cambridge: Cambridge University Press.

Winston, P.H. (1975). Learning structural descriptions from examples. In P.H. Winston (Ed.), *The psychology of computer vision.* New York: McGraw-Hill.

Winston, P.H. (1984). *Artificial intelligence* (2nd ed.). Reading, MA: Addison-Wesley.

Wise, M. N. (1979). The mutual embrace of electricity and magnetism. *Science, 203,* 1310–1318.

Wittgenstein, L. (1953). *Philosophical investigations.* New York: Macmillan.

Woodworth, R.S., & Schlosberg, H. (1954). *Experimental psychology* (3rd ed.). New York: Holt, Rinehart & Winston.

Woodworth, R.S. & Sells, S.B. (1935). An atmosphere effect in formal syllogistic reasoning. *Journal of Experimental Psychology, 18,* 451–460.

Wos, L. (1988). *Automated reasoning: 33 basic research problems.* Englewood Cliffs, NJ: Prentice-Hall.

Author Index

Subject Index

A

Abduction, 66, 83
  See also Induction
Abstraction, 37–39, 63
Algorithms, See Computer programs
Analogies, 133, 149–151
Architecture, 13–14, 121 et seq, 127–129
Arithmetic, xiii, 5, 56, 122, 153
  See also Recursive functions
Artificial intelligence, xv–xvi, 9, 11–12, 37,
    48–54, 71 et seq, 109
Artistic creation, 115, 118 et seq, 128 et
    seq, 162, 166
Associations, xiii–xv
Atmosphere effect, in syllogistic reasoning,
    xv–xvii, 36
Automata, See Machines
Automated reasoning, 8–12, 48–54
Availability, of beliefs or rules, 20, 26–27,
    67–68, 70, 86, 109, 112–113, 127–128

B

Bars, in musical notation, 141–142
Bass lines, in music, 145–147
Behaviorism, 63
Beliefs, and thinking, 2, 15, 19–20, 23–25,
    59, 112, 154 et seq

Biases, See Atmosphere effect, Availability,
    Beliefs, Figure of syllogisms
Binary arithmetic, 122
Boolean algebra, 48, 71–73, 78–81, 125–126
Brain, xi, xiii, 121, 161

C

Calculation, xiii–xv
Calculus, See Logic
Cause, concept of, 103–106
Censor, 23
Changes, in beliefs or concepts, 154 et seq
Chaos, and chaotic systems, 120
Chernobyl disaster, 56–57, 59, 113
Chess, xvi, 73, 124, 125
Children's thinking, 25–26, 32, 73, 76, 87,
    108, 151 et seq
Choice, 120–121, 123
Chomsky hierarchy, 122–123
Chord sequences, 134–140
Church's thesis, 91, 116, 154
Cognitive architecture, 13–14, 121 et seq,
    127–129
Cognitive neuropsychology, xiii
Cognitive science, xvi–xviii, 165
Common sense, See Everyday thinking,
    Knowledge, Practical inference
Compilation, of programs and subconcepts,
    108–109, 128, 147, 155, 162

183